The
Investor's
Mindset

Ben Le Fort

The Investor's Mindset

ANALYZE MARKETS.
INVEST STRATEGICALLY.
MINIMIZE RISK.
MAXIMIZE RETURNS.

"A refreshing , much-needed game plan."
Tim Denning, finance and personal development writer

Editor Florence Ward
Designer James McKeag
Senior Production Editor Jennifer Murray
Senior Production Controller Louise Minihane
Managing Editor Pete Jorgensen
Managing Art Editor Jo Connor
Publishing Director Mark Searle

Designed for DK by Thelma-Jane Robb.
DK would also like to thank Clare Sayer for copyediting, Claire Nottage for proofreading and Vanessa Bird for indexing.

First American Edition, 2023
Published in the United States by DK Publishing
1745 Broadway, 20th Floor, New York, NY 10019

Page design copyright © 2023 Dorling Kindersley Limited
DK, a Division of Penguin Random House LLC
23 24 25 26 27 10 9 8 7 6 5 4 3 2
003–332483–July/2023

DK books are available at special discounts when purchased in bulk for sales promotions, premiums, fund-raising, or educational use. For details, contact:
DK Publishing Special Markets,
1745 Broadway, 20th Floor, New York, NY 10019
SpecialSales@dk.com

Printed and bound in China.

For the curious
www.dk.com

Picture Credits
The publisher would like to thank the following for their kind permission to reproduce their photographs:
(Key: a-above; b-below/bottom; c-center; f-far; l-left; r-right; t-top)
11 Getty Images: New York Daily News. 17 Getty Images: Contour / Emma McIntyre / Staff.
25 Getty Images: John Lamparski / WireImage. 31 Getty Images: Hulton Archive / Stringer.
36 Getty Images: David Yellen / Corbis. 55 Getty Images: Juergen Frank / Contour RA / Corbis.
64 Alamy Stock Photo: Chronicle. 70 Alamy Stock Photo: UPI / Kevin Dietsch.
75 Getty Images: The Chronicle Collection / Steve Liss. 84 Getty Images: Paul Morigi / WireImage.
90 Getty Images: Andreas Rentz / Staff. 97 Getty Images: Samir Hussein / WireImage.
99 Getty Images: Jin Lee / Bloomberg. 103 Getty Images: George Karger / Pix / Michael Ochs Archives.
122 Getty Images: Vera Anderson / WireImage. 130 Getty Images: WireImage / Mark Sullivan / Stringer.
138 Getty Images: Neilson Barnard / Staff. 150 Getty Images: Roberto Finizio
All other images © Dorling Kindersley

Contents

Is this book for you?

To invest successfully does not require a stratospheric IQ, unusual business insights, or inside information. What's needed is a sound intellectual framework for making decisions and the ability to keep emotions from corroding the framework.

These are the words of investing legend Warren Buffett, and they summarize the mission statement of this book.

Few myths have done more damage to the ability of the ordinary person to build wealth than the lie that you need to be an 'expert' to succeed as an investor. In the past, the widespread belief in this myth only benefited those 'experts' who worked in the financial services industry. The more people who believed that hiring these masters of the investing universe was the only way to get ahead, the higher the fees they were able to charge. In recent years, another group has benefited from this myth: financial influencers or 'finfluencers'. Social media has allowed the loudest people in the room to grab the megaphone and command attention. This has led to a rise in investing advice from colorful online personalities that want to 'teach' you how to invest. Often these teachings involve big claims about returns that cannot be verified and are not based in reality, all while minimizing—or being completely ignorant to—the very real risks involved with what they preach.

In Part One of this book, I will take a wrecking ball to the myth that you need to be an expert to be a successful investor. As Buffett points out, the first thing you need is a sound intellectual framework for making investment decisions. By the end of Part One, you will understand how to build a simple and properly diversified portfolio that will allow you to build long-term wealth without having to check in on your portfolio every day.

Building an investment portfolio is a lot simpler than you might think. The hard part about investing is that it requires a lifetime of consistency. Wealth is built over thousands of small decisions that take place over a lifetime. But all that hard work can be undone with one very bad decision at the worst time.

The second key point that Buffett makes is that you need to 'keep emotions from corroding the framework'. That is why in Part Two of this book, you will learn how to adopt 'The Investor's Mindset.' The chapters will cover harmful cognitive biases that all people suffer from that drive bad investing decisions, psychological characteristics leading to the best investment outcomes, financial habits to help you stay invested for the long run, and how to tune out the loudest voices on social media who use fearmongering tactics (FOMO and YOLO) to grab hold of your attention and your wallet. An investment in this book will give you the knowledge you need to build a portfolio and empower you with the tools to build the investor's mindset that is required to stick with your investment plan through good times and bad. If you are ready to get started, flip the page. Let's get going.

Part One

The Myths

Investing & the internet

Here's an interesting fact: 91% of Gen Z and 75% of millennials rely on social media to get information about how to invest their money.[1]

Statistics like this shouldn't come as a surprise to anyone. We live in an increasingly digital world, and younger generations spend more of their lives on social media. If you can find a spouse online, it stands to reason that you can find helpful investment advice online too. There is a lot of helpful investment advice on the internet. The problem is that we are drowning in an endless ocean of online content.

To make matters worse, most of the content shown to us is decided by an algorithm. These algorithms don't promote accurate or quality content. Social media platforms that rely on advertisement revenue and algorithms value one metric above all: engagement, or in other words, keeping you on the app for as long as possible. The longer they keep you on the app, the more ads they can show you. So, the algorithm serves up content you are most likely to click on.

That's why you should never assume that someone with a large following on social media is an expert in the subject they are discussing, or that they have your best interests at heart. This is especially true when it comes to the investing advice you find online.

Online financial influencers, or 'finfluencers', understand that these social media algorithms reward engagement. This gives them a powerful financial incentive to produce investment content that will grab your attention. Here are three ingredients commonly found in a viral investment video.

1. *An over-the-top claim like, 'WE ARE ABOUT TO ENTER A GREAT DEPRESSION!' Inevitably, they provide little or no evidence to back up their bold claim.*
2. *A solution to the problem they just convinced you is real. They tell you exactly what you should do to avoid losing all your money.*
3. *A sales pitch, for example, 'Buy my course where I teach you how to trade stocks. Normally it sells for $10,000, but you can get it today for $500!'*

This is all very sales 101. As we will explore later in the book, anyone on the internet who claims they can teach you how to pick stocks is full of it. Most professional Wall Street investment fund managers can't consistently pick stocks that outperform. These are people with an army of Ivy League-trained analysts and more money than a small European country, and most of them fail to pick winning stocks consistently. But the 23-year-old TikTok star who started investing eight months ago? They'll have you believe that not only can they pick the winning stocks, but they can also teach you how to do it too.

You might be thinking, how do they get away with this? How can someone with no experience or credentials sell you a course on picking stocks or trade options? Ironically, it's precisely because they have no credentials that they can get away with it. Finfluencers are not financial professionals, which means they don't have an obligation to act in your best interest. There are no laws and regulations that dictate what is

"I hate to see innocent,
misguided people get hurt."

*Muriel Siebert, the first woman to own a seat on
the New York Stock Exchange*

acceptable in the world of online investment content. In a world dominated by algorithms, the best storytellers will always win the most attention, but it doesn't mean you should listen to them.

We all need a strong financial bullshit filter

A 2022 study titled 'Individual differences in susceptibility to financial bullshit' examined people's ability to tell the difference between helpful advice and 'financial bullshit'.[2] The researchers defined financial bullshit, the kind commonly experienced by consumers when seeking out financial products as services, as 'pseudo-profound bullshit, in the form of empty talk, lingo, and jargon'.

They were also able to identify the characteristics of a person most likely to fall for financial bullshit: young, male, on a high income, scored low when tested on financial knowledge, and overconfident.

We all need to keep our guard up when consuming investment content online. Over the next few chapters, we will review critical investing concepts you'll need to know in order to tell the difference between legitimate investment opportunities and financial scams. In Section 2 of this book, we will address the issue of overconfidence, focusing on how it can hurt investors and how to thread the needle so that you can remain confident but level-headed as an investor.

The Dogecoin Hustle

No discussion about financial bullshit is complete without mentioning crypto.

Dogecoin started as a joke cryptocurrency. This was until Elon Musk started tweeting about Dogecoin and promoting it to his followers. On 3 February 2021, Dogecoin was worth $0.037. The following day Musk tweeted a simple message: 'Dogecoin is the people's crypto.' Within 72 hours, the price of Dogecoin increased by 123%.

The internet became captivated by Musk's enthusiasm for Dogecoin. Suddenly it was no longer a joke but a speculative asset that people were taking very seriously. Headlines started popping up about people who poured their life savings into Dogecoin and became overnight millionaires.

The Dogecoin mania peaked on 7 May 2021, the day before Elon Musk appeared on Saturday Night Live. At its peak, Dogecoin had increased by over 1,850% in just over three months. But the bubble burst after Musk jokingly referred to Dogecoin as a 'hustle' during his appearance on the show and over the next 13 months, Dogecoin lost over 93% of its value. Those who invested at the top of the Dogecoin bubble lost big.

The Dogecoin mania is a textbook example of how investment bubbles form. In a 2021 paper titled 'The Ex Ante Likelihood of Bubbles', Alex Chinco developed a framework to explain how likely a bubble is to occur.[3] Chinco found that bubbles are most likely to occur when 'increases in past returns make excited speculators relatively more persuasive to their peers.'

If Dogecoin goes up in price, it's easier for a Dogecoin speculator to convince people that it will continue to go up. Chinco also found that the more a speculative asset like Dogecoin receives positive media coverage, the more likely that asset is to grow into a bubble. Every headline in early 2021 about 'Dogecoin millionaires' made it easier for people to convince themselves that they should jump on the bandwagon and invest.

Remember: The investments you should be most skeptical about are the ones with the loudest supporters.

Financial time travel

Saving and investing money is like writing a check to your future self. If you save $100 today, that means at some point in the future, maybe one month from now, maybe 50 years from now, your future self will have that $100, plus whatever interest you have built up along the way.

Time travel does exist, but it has two rules. Firstly, you can only transport money (not people) through time. Secondly, you can only send money into the future. Sadly, we cannot change our financial past, only our financial future, by choosing to save and invest.

Now that we are clear on the rules of financial time travel, you need to think about how far into the future you want to send your money. This is the part where you need to understand the difference between saving your money and investing your money. If you want to send your money into the not-too-distant future, you need to save your money. Money that you might need any time in the next few weeks or even the next few years needs to be saved, not invested.

Saving your money means putting it aside for short-term financial goals

A financial emergency fund is a great example of a short-term goal where you should save rather than invest. An emergency fund means you have access to cash to pay your bills in the event of a financial emergency, like losing your job. Since a financial emergency could strike at any moment, you don't want to take any risk with your emergency fund. That means using a short-term savings vehicle like a savings account. It's boring, and your money will barely accumulate any interest, but it will be there for you when you need it.

Here are five other examples of savings goals, where you are transporting your money into the not-too-distant future and therefore do not want to take any risks.

1. **Money you need in the next 30-days:** *Your checking account (or current account in the UK) is where your paychecks are deposited and where your bill payments and savings withdrawals come from. Think of your checking account like an airport with money constantly flying in and out every day. Like an airport, the money does not live in your checking account. The checking account's purpose is to park that money before it departs for its final destination.*

2. **Vacations:** *If you love to travel, then you should have a vacation fund.*

3. **Home repairs:** *If you own a home, you should have a house fund where you set aside money to cover the annual maintenance cost.*

4. **Car maintenance:** *For car costs like repairs, servicing costs, and buying new cars in the future, you'll need to set aside money in a car fund.*

4. **Expensive life events you know are coming:** *For example, if you are expecting or trying to have a baby, it makes sense to put money aside in a safe place to help pay for the mountain of baby start-up costs like cribs, strollers, and diapers. Maybe you're planning to buy your first home in the next few years; if so, you're going to need to have cash set aside for the down payment.*

Why you should never invest short-term money

The stock market is a dangerous place to keep money you need for short-term financial goals. The stock market is volatile, which means it can drop in value very far and very fast. In 1931 the S&P 500, which tracks the 500 largest public companies in the US, lost nearly 44% of its value. On a single day in 1987, the stock market dropped 22%. Volatility means things can get ugly in the blink of an eye. If you only need to transport money a short distance into the future for something very important to your day-to-day life, a savings account is a far better option than the stock market.

Investing your money means putting it aside for long-term financial goals

It's time to rev up the DeLorean and talk about sending your money into the distant future. If you want to take $100 and send it to your future self five months from now, a savings account will do fine. But if you want to take that $100 and send it to your future self 40 years from now, you need to invest it.

There's this pesky thing called inflation, which means the price of things we want to buy goes up most years and to make matters worse, the interest your savings account pays is unlikely to keep pace with inflation. That's why we invest in riskier assets like the stock market, which have a long track record of outpacing inflation.

If you're lucky, investing $100 today will allow you to spend more than $100 in the future, even after taking inflation into account. You take money today, throw it in the investing time machine, and a few decades later you meet up with that money to buy things without relying on a paycheck, also known as retirement planning.

"The thing that I learned early on is you really need to set goals in your life, both short-term and long-term, just like you do in business. Having that long-term goal will enable you to have a plan on how to achieve it. We apply these skills in business, yet when it comes to ourselves, we rarely apply them."

Denise Morrison, former CEO of Campbell Soup Company

Retirement planning is an outdated term and conjures images of sitting in a stuffy boardroom, sitting across from a financial planner who is trying to sell you expensive investment products. Let's replace the word 'retirement' with 'financial independence'. One way of defining financial independence as having enough money so that work becomes optional. Retirement is for grandparents; financial independence is for everyone.

If your goal is to one day reach financial independence, then you are going to need to invest some of your money. Again, you have inflation to thank for this. Over long periods of time, even small amounts of inflation will eat away at the value of money. Here's how long it takes for different rates of annual inflation to cut the value of your money in half.

- *2% inflation → 36 years*
- *3% inflation → 24 years*
- *4% inflation → 18 years*
- *5% inflation → 14.5 years*

What this means is that if inflation was running at 3% and you put all your money in a savings account that only earned 1% per year, the value of your savings would be cut in half after 36 years. Time destroys everything, even money. This is the basic reason you need to invest; so that the money you put in your time machine today earns enough interest so that you can buy the same (or more) amount of goods several decades down the road. The benefit of investing in the stock market is that it is likely to outperform inflation in the long run. The elephant in the room is that investing involves risk, and that makes most people very uncomfortable, usually because they are focused on the short term. In the short run, there is a good chance your investments will go down.

However, if you are focused on the long run, investing in the stock market isn't so scary. Here's a comforting fact: at the time I write this, nobody in history has ever lost money by buying the entire US stock market and sitting on it for at least 20 years.[1]

How do you 'buy the entire' stock market? By using index funds that aim to replicate the performance of a stock market index. If that sounds like a bunch of gobbledygook, don't worry. We will cover everything you need to know about index funds and how to invest in the stock market in Chapter 5. For now, think of it this way: index funds = buying the entire stock market.

Thinking in the long run removes the need to freak out about what's happening day-to-day in the stock market. If you started investing in 2023 and don't plan on using that money for 30 years, ask yourself one simple question; are you worried about what happened in the stock market in 1993? No? Then you shouldn't be worried about what happens in the stock market in 2023, either. However, most investors sabotage their investment success at some point along the way, typically for one of three reasons.

1. *They get nervous about an 'impending market crash,' so they sell their investments.*
2. *They get bored and sell their investments, then jump on whatever hot new investment idea is trending on social media, just before said trending investment is about to blow up.*
3. *They get greedy and use dangerous tools like leverage (debt) in an attempt to make more money, but it blows up in their face.*

The idea of investing and building wealth can feel intimidating to many people, but I am here to tell you that building wealth is a straightforward three-step process. Let's break each step down.

Step 1: Spend less than you earn

The basic arithmetic of building wealth is simple: your income must always be higher than your living expenses. So then the question becomes, should you focus on lowering your expenses or increasing your income?

For most of us, it's not possible to just 'decide' that you want to earn more money and instantly double your income. You can, however, decide you want to lower your cost of living and spend an afternoon creating a new budget that reduces your spending. If you have monthly subscriptions that you aren't using regularly (if at all!) canceling them is a great place to start cutting your spending. However, you can only cut your living expenses so far without going below what you need to live your best life, so in the long run, focus on ways to increase your income.

Step 2: Put your money to work

I have some good news and some bad news. The good news is that all long-term index fund investors can easily become millionaires. The bad news is it will take a long time and, if done properly, is a pretty boring process.

Here's a straightforward example that illustrates how simple it is to build wealth when you buy the entire stock market and hold it for a few decades.

Let's say you . . .
- *Start with $0*
- *Invest $500 per month into index funds*
- *Increase the amount you save by the rate of inflation each year*
- *Have an average 6% return on investments*

The results? That monthly $500 investment would make you a millionaire in 35 years.

I should mention that there is nothing magical about having $1 million; it's simply a large round number that is nice to use in an example like this. True wealth is not about how much money you have; it's about how much money you have relative to your living expenses. If you are happy spending $50,000 per year, then $1 million will mean a lot more to you than someone who needs $250,000 per year.

Step 3: Be patient

Building wealth is simple. Anybody can do it by earning more than they spend and investing in index funds. But just because something is simple does not make it easy. Don't be fooled: building wealth is hard, which is why so few people do it.

The hard part is that it can be a slow, non-linear process. You need discipline and patience. To be honest, it will probably take decades—not years—to build enough wealth for you to fund your lifestyle from your investments. (Sorry, there are no 'to the moon' get-rich-quick ideas in this book.)

The good news is that building wealth is not like turning on a light switch. You don't spend 20 years being poor, and then suddenly someone flicks on the lights, and you're wealthy. If you stay consistent with steps 1 and 2, you begin building more wealth each year. The more wealth you build, the more flexibility you have to live life on your terms.

A bonus step!

Building wealth is a slow process, but that does not mean there isn't anything you can do to speed things up. Here's a simple formula.

INCOME — EXPENSES — MONEY FOR SHORT TERM SAVINGS GOALS = INVESTABLE MONEY

If you want to speed up the wealth-building process, you need more investible money and the only way to increase your investable money is to widen the gap between your income and expenses. If you've been tracking your spending and budgeting, then there probably isn't too much left you can do on the expense side of the equation. This leaves us with an obvious conclusion: the only way to speed up the wealth-building process is to make more money. You might ask for a raise at work, switch companies for a better salary, learn a new valuable skill, or start a side hustle.

Slow and steady: the story of Ronald Read

Here's a depressing statistic: 42% of the adult population in the US has $0 invested in the stock market.[3]

A critical question for this large group of people is, 'why not?' A 2018 study by James Choi and Adriana Robertson surveyed 1,013 people to better understand how people view the stock market.[4] They also surveyed people who don't invest in the stock market and asked them why they don't invest. The number one answer was that people did not believe they had enough money to start investing.

If you believe investing is only for people making six-figure salaries, then let me tell you the story of Ronald Read. Ronald spent his career working as a janitor and a gas station attendant. These are not exactly the jobs most people think of when they envision a millionaire stock market investor. But that is exactly what Ronald was.

In June 2014, Ronald died at the age of 92. As his estate was being settled, his friends and family were shocked to learn that Ronald had left behind an $8 million fortune, consisting largely of investments in the stock market. Ronald never made a fat six-figure salary or received a massive inheritance. He didn't work at a tech company or sell a start-up. He worked blue-collar jobs, lived a frugal lifestyle, invested early and often, held on to his investments, and had the good fortune to live to be 95 years old. If Ronald can do it, so can you.

Personal finance for investors

Y ou've probably heard of the phrase 'buy low and sell high'. The idea is that the easiest way to make money in the stock market is to buy when prices are low and sell when prices are high. Buy low and sell high is the kind of investment advice that sounds good on paper but can be dangerous to follow through on.

It implies that you know when stocks are 'cheap', when they are 'expensive', and what will happen to stock prices in the future. While there are valuation metrics to determine if a stock is expensive or cheap, as we will cover in Chapter 5, knowing what will happen with stock prices in the future is a near impossibility for anyone who doesn't own a crystal ball. A more useful investing phrase for long-term investing success is to 'buy low and buy high, and continue buying until you hit your financial goals.'

Over the long term, the stock market tends to go up, but the road is very bumpy. Investors often lose money when they mistake a bump in the road for a sinkhole and sell their investments to avoid an 'impending market crash' that never happens. Even if the stock market does crash into the kind of hole we experienced in the Global Financial Crisis of 2008, the solution for a well-diversified investor is to simply do nothing.

Investors who manage to ride out a market crash without selling see their paper losses reverse back into gains as the market recovers. Those who sell after a market crash turn paper losses into real losses and permanently destroy the wealth they had previously built up.

There are two primary reasons an investor would choose to sell at the bottom after a market crash: a fear-driven decision to panic sell, and poor financial planning. Much of this book is dedicated to developing the investor's mindset, one that will help you avoid making investment decisions that are driven by fear. In this chapter, we will review some of the fundamental financial planning decisions you can make to minimize the odds of ever being forced to sell your portfolio at the worst possible time. Even if you have nerves of steel, if you find yourself in a position where you have no income and no cash savings, you may have no choice but to sell your investments at a loss. After all, you still need to put food on the table. Long-term investing is impossible without financial stability.

An emergency fund can help you invest well

An emergency fund just means having cash set aside to cover two types of situations.

1. *When you incur large, unexpected financial costs such as when your car breaks down and needs expensive repairs, or even replacing.*
2. *To cover all of your essential living expenses if you lose your job or have your income reduced dramatically.*

If you live in the United States and don't have medical insurance, a trip to the hospital can be financially devastating. If you don't have an emergency fund, you're left with two options for paying medical bills: going into debt or liquidating a portion of your investment portfolio.

"I was desperate to understand money. Not to make it, to understand it. I wanted to know how it worked, and I wanted to know so that I would have enough and would be able to make good financial decisions."

Mellody Hobson, co-CEO of Ariel Investments

And if the due date on that medical bill coincides with a stock market crash, your problems will compound.

Stock markets tend to crash during economic recessions and during recessions companies try to cut their costs. Most major corporations' largest expense is the people they employ, so the first place they look to cut costs is your salary. This means there is a high probability that you could lose your job at the same time as your investments are taking a beating. Even if you are the most rational investor in the world and you know you shouldn't sell when markets are down, you might not have a choice if you lose your job and you don't have an adequate emergency fund in place.

The first question about an emergency fund, is how much money you should have in it? The truth is that it depends on your personal circumstances. For example, someone living in a two-income household might not need as big an emergency fund as someone in a single-income household. Another factor to consider is how long it might take you to find a comparable job. If you work in a field where the average job search takes six months, that's a pretty good indicator of how big your emergency fund should be.

Most financial experts recommend having three to six months of living expenses in your emergency fund, and that would seem to be a reasonable starting point. From there, you can choose to add or subtract from that amount, depending on your particular circumstances. A strong emergency fund will minimize the odds of being forced to sell your investments at the worst possible time.

Don't listen to finfluencers who tell you to invest your emergency fund

Finfluencers love contrarian thinking when it comes to money because challenging mainstream thinking is one of the easiest ways to jack up engagement with a post.

Sometimes, contrarian thinking leads to better outcomes. Twenty years ago, the consensus thinking was that first-time home buyers should have a down payment of at least 20% of the purchase price before buying a home. In today's environment of sky-high house prices, that figure is unattainable for most first-time buyers. Many financially savvy investors now realize that investing their disposable income instead can help them build wealth quicker. But often, contrarian financial advice is lazy and does little more than telling the reader what they want to hear rather than what they need to hear. A prime example of this is telling you that you should invest the money in your emergency fund rather than leave it in cash.

Keeping money in a cash account feels like a bit of a scam because of how little interest they pay, which means we are ready to listen when someone tells us it's okay to invest our emergency fund instead of leaving it where it is. It's like being told that eating candy is good for us. Well, I am here to tell you to put the candy away and eat some broccoli.

Your emergency fund is not an investment. Its purpose is not to make you money. Your emergency fund is an insurance policy and its purpose is to provide you with risk-free access to cash in case you lose your job or incur a large, unexpected cost. You keep an emergency fund for the same reason you buy house insurance: if an unforeseen negative event happens, you're protected. But like with any insurance policy, you pay a premium; in this case the premium you pay is the difference between the interest you'll earn on the cash in your savings account, and the returns you would have received had you invested the money.

Build your financial fortress

As an investor, you should think of financial planning like building a financial fortress. In the center of the fortress is your investment portfolio. Outside the gates of your financial fortress are the economic barbarians; market crashes, recessions, medical bills, and any other nasty financial setbacks that could force you to sell your investments.

Your emergency fund is the most important wall in your financial fortress, but think of it as your last line of defense. Having an emergency fund in place can give you peace of mind but actually having to use an emergency fund to pay the rent or put food on the table is alarming. If you have no income and just three months' worth of living expenses in your emergency fund, every day that goes by is like watching the sand fall in an hourglass. The best emergency fund is one you never have to use.

So how do you avoid ever having to rely on your emergency fund? The answer is to put up more walls to protect your financial fortress.

If your emergency fund is the first wall around your money fortress, then minimizing your spending is the second wall. By reducing your spending, you can make your emergency fund last even longer. If you have $24,000 in an emergency fund and you spend $8,000 per month, you can go three months without earning any income. If you can learn to live on $6,000 per month, that same $24,000 will last you four months; if you can halve your spending to $4,000 per month, that three months' worth of funds will last you twice as long.

The next wall defending your financial fortress is diversifying your income streams. The best financial defense will always be to have a monthly income that exceeds your monthly expenses, and you can achieve this through a low cost of living and a solid 9-5 job. But with a 9-5 job, all your eggs are in one basket and if you lose your job, you instantly enter the undesirable situation of living off your emergency fund. As explained, cutting your expenses can help you stretch that emergency fund longer, but the real trick is to diversify your income with a side hustle—either a business or a second job. If you have a side hustle that can cover your basic living expenses, then even if you lose your job, you aren't forced to touch your emergency fund or your investment portfolio.

The final wall protecting your money fortress is your 9-5 job or primary income source. The problem most people have is that their main paycheck is the only thing protecting their portfolio from being sold off in a pinch. By reviewing and cutting unneeded expenses, building a strong emergency fund, and adding a second income stream you can minimize the odds that you would need to sell your investments to pay the bills if you were to lose your job.

Worry more about a personal recession than a national recession

So we've looked at some of the ways in which you can protect your finances from an economic recession. Let's take this concept to the next level. While it is important to be prepared for a national recession—where the unemployment rate rises and the stock market goes down—it's much more important to prepare for a personal recession.

A good financial decision for me may not be a good financial decision for you. Everything depends on your personal circumstances, goals, and risk tolerance. Here's another truism: economics is personal too. The impact the next recession will have on you will be radically different from the impact it has on your cousin, your boss, or your neighbor. In every booming economy, there are millions of people who are living in poverty. If you have to choose between putting food on the table or paying the electricity bill, what do you care if the unemployment rate is historically low?

On the flip side, many people during the Great Depression of the 1930s and the 2008 financial crisis became wealthier. When it comes to managing money during a recession, the state of your personal finances is infinitely more important than the national unemployment rate.

Economists have very technical definitions of what constitutes a recession at the national level, but it is generally defined as a period of prolonged negative GDP (gross domestic product) growth, weakening labor markets, and lower levels of investment and spending. However, a personal recession can be triggered by all sorts of events that have nothing to do with national GDP:

- *You get fired*
- *You get sick or injured*
- *Your car breaks down*
- *Your roof blows off*
- *You get divorced*
- *You make a terrible money decision (like buying a boat)*

The person who is always preparing for a personal recession is the one who will be in the best position to make it through a national recession.

"Buy when everyone else is selling, and hold on until everyone else is buying.'

J. Paul Getty, American oil tycoon

A recession can be a financial opportunity

Getty put his philosophy into action after the 1929 stock market crash. When most people struggled to put food on the table, and large corporations were on the verge of bankruptcy, Getty did what few other people did at the time: he started buying up companies left and right. His investment of choice was oil companies, which were trading at a fraction of the cost before the Great Depression. He once said that buying these companies at such a discounted price was 'the opportunity of a lifetime.'

You don't have to be a genius to realize that buying stocks after a market crash is an amazing opportunity to build future wealth. The problem is, however, that the time when stocks are cheap is the time when most people are struggling to make ends meet, let alone invest in stocks.

The reason Getty was able to buy up these oil companies for peanuts and be regarded as a business legend is that he was in a financial position to buy when everyone else was forced to sell. Getty was already a millionaire by the time the stock market crashed in 1929 (bear in mind that this was when $1 million was worth more than $17 million in today's dollars).

You certainly don't need $17 million or even $1 million to be in a position to buy when others are selling. What you do need is to be in a stable financial position when a recession hits and stocks go on sale. So keep working on strengthening the walls of your financial fortress by diversifying income streams, paying off debt, building an emergency fund, and keeping your living expenses in check. Every crisis is an opportunity, but only if your financial position is strong enough to weather the storm.

How not to invest in the stock market

Before we talk about how rational thinkers invest their money, it's worth taking some time to discuss how not to invest your money.

The financial media and online finfluencers present investing as both essential for your financial future (true) and incredibly complicated (false). As we reviewed in Chapter 2, investing is important for your financial future. However, I will show you in Chapters 5 and 6 that investing can be a very simple process if you let it. And it can (and should) be learned by either piecing together a series of free resources or paying a small fee to have everything you need to know packaged together, like the book you are reading right now.

In this chapter I will review the most common investing strategies promoted by finfluencers and certain corners of the financial services industry looking to make money from you. I'll throw some cold water on each of these strategies in the form of data, logical thinking, and research.

Stock picking

Picking and choosing individual stocks in an attempt to 'beat the market' is something promoted by finfluencers, mainstream financial media, and large swathes of the financial services industry. For finfluencers and the financial media, talking about the daily happenings in financial markets and which stocks you should buy and which stocks you should sell provides endless fresh content for them to serve up. The longer they can hold your attention, the more stuff they can sell you. Many financial services firms justify their high fees by touting their ability to choose the right stocks at the right time.

If someone could show me credible evidence that picking stocks is a reliable way to beat the market and is something that can be taught to others, I'd be all for it, except that the evidence does not exist. Let's review the evidence around picking stocks so that you can understand how worthless almost every single 'hot stock tip' truly is.

What the stock pickers don't tell you

There's this thing in finance that the stock pickers really don't want you to pay attention to: it's called the efficient market hypothesis (EMH). It was put forward back in the 1960s by an economist named Eugene Fama; basically, it says that the price of any given stock in the market reflects all available information about that company.

If a company already has all publicly available information baked into its stock price, then picking and choosing stocks is no different from throwing darts at a board while wearing a blindfold. If markets are efficient, the only way to consistently pick and choose stocks that outperform is to have a crystal ball, or insider information about a company. (As an aside; you can be thrown into jail for trading on insider information; if they did it to Martha Stewart, you can bet they'll do it to you too.)

In 2013, Fama won the Nobel Prize in Economics for his research on efficient markets. However, even Fama would admit that the stock market is not 100% efficient 100% of the time. Even if markets are not perfectly efficient, they are efficient enough that the odds of successfully picking and choosing individual stocks to outperform the market are abysmal.

If you want to know how difficult it is to pick and choose stocks that will outperform the average return of the stock market, let's have a look at how professional stock pickers who run billion-dollar investment funds on Wall Street do it. Surely, if anyone can beat the market consistently over time, it's these high-powered investment fund managers who have unlimited resources and an army of analysts and research staff at their disposal, right?

Wrong. Data from the S&P Dow Jones Indices shows that over the past 10 years.[1]

- *83% of European investment fund managers underperformed the S&P Europe 350*
- *83% of Canadian investment fund managers underperformed the TSX*
- *86% of Mexican investment fund managers underperformed the S&P/ BMV IRT*
- *87% of Brazilian investment fund managers underperformed the S&P Brazil BMI*
- *79% of Japanese investment fund managers underperformed the S&P/ TOPIX 150*
- *84% of Australian investment fund managers underperformed the S&P/ ASX 200*

Across the globe, the vast majority of investment fund managers fail to pick the right stocks to outperform the local stock market that they are measured against. So ask yourself this: if the top investment professionals in the world can't pick stocks, what are the odds that a 23-year-old YouTuber can teach you how to do it?

Even 'superstar' investment fund managers struggle to beat the market over time

Ken Heebner was one of the hottest investment fund managers of the 2000s. Heebner's investment fund, CGM Focus, basically throws diversification out the window by making concentrated bets on a small number of individual stocks. From 2000-2007 those concentrated bets paid off as Heebner's fund increased by 479% from January 2000 to December 2007. In 2007 the fund returned a whopping 80% gain in a single year.

But as they say, all good things come to an end. The financial crisis of 2007–2009 saw the fund lose 64% of its value from December 2007 to March 2009. As of 1 August 2022, the fund was still down over 30% from its peak in 2007.

Meanwhile, the S&P 500 was up over 170% over the same period. In both stock picking and in life, Father Time is undefeated.

Day trading

The best way to describe day trading is that it's like stock picking but on steroids. Not only do day traders pick individual stocks, they quickly flip (or sell) them for another stock in an attempt to make a quick buck.

Both finfluencers and discount online investment brokerages like Robinhood have financial incentives for you to day trade stocks. For the finfluencers, it's an opportunity to—you guessed it—sell you their online course or program. They will tell you about how they got rich day trading and how you can do the same if you simply follow their secret trading strategy. Please do not waste your time and money on such nonsense. Courses teaching you to day trade are the height of financial bullshit. If this person has actually unlocked a secret code to beat the market, why has a giant Wall Street bank like Goldman Sachs not written a blank check to either hire this person or license their market-beating trading strategy for an ungodly amount of money?

The reality of day trading

Every finfluencer selling a stock trading course will tout their amazing market-beating returns. The problem is that you have no way of verifying their claims, forcing you to simply take them at their word.

The evidence we do have about the income that day traders earn is quite damning. A 2019 paper titled 'Day Trading for a Living?' written by Fernando Chague and colleagues studied the returns of day traders in Brazil over a three-year period. Here are the headline results of the study.[2]

- 97% of day traders who were active longer than 300 days lost money.
- 1.1% earned more than the Brazilian minimum wage.
- 0.5% earned more than the initial salary of a bank teller.

By those measures, the best-case scenario of day trading is that you can make the starting salary of a bank teller but without any of the job security or benefits. You also have a 97% chance of wasting time and money.

"There's no statistical evidence that human beings have an ability to move in and out of the markets effectively. It's next to impossible."

- *John W. Rogers, Jr, Co-CEO of Ariel Capital Management*

Can someone learn to trade stocks?

Let's assume that the finfluencer selling you an online trading course is in the top 0.1% of all day traders and does make a little bit of money through day trading. There is another hurdle they must clear before selling a day trading course makes any sense. Can they teach you how to be a successful day trader? Because if the answer is no, then it does not matter if someone is an incredible day trader if it isn't a skill that can be learned. It would be like LeBron James selling you a course on how to grow to 6 foot 8. Just because he is tall does not mean you can 'learn' to be tall too.

Chague examined the question of whether trading is a skill that can be learned and found 'no evidence of learning' among the day traders in their sample.[3] Here's a quote from the paper that acts as the final nail in the coffin of online trading courses: 'It is virtually impossible for individuals to day trade for a living, contrary to what course providers claim.'

Options trading

Here's an example of the kind of financial bullshit I see way too often on Twitter: 'Here's how I make $XX per month in passive income using call options.' If you see someone tweet something like this, your best move is to block them. Let's start with a basic explanation of call and put options.

- *Call options allow you to buy a stock at a specified price within a predetermined time range. If the stock does not reach the specified price, the option expires and becomes worthless. To buy an option, you must pay a premium. If you don't use the option, you lose the premium.*
- *Put options allow you to sell a stock at a specified price within a predetermined time range. Put simply (I could not resist the pun), a put option is the opposite of a call option.*

Think of it this way: if you wanted to make a bet that the price of a stock is going to go up, you would buy a call option, whereas if you wanted to make a bet that the price of a stock is going to go down, you would buy a put option. I am very intentionally using the term 'bet' rather than 'invest' because that's what most finfluencers are doing when they trade options.

At the beginning of the COVID-19 pandemic there were no live sports, and millions of people were stuck at home with nothing to do. The huge numbers of people that would typically spend their money on sports gambling turned to betting their money in the stock market. However, for many of these speculators, simply betting on individual stocks did not provide enough risk for their taste. To get the thrill they were seeking, they turned to options trading, which sent trading volumes to an all-time high during the early days of the pandemic.[4] Like with sports gambling, options trading allows thrill seekers to quickly hit the jackpot—or lose big—by making one big bet.

The reality of options trading

Much like with trading stocks, the first question we should ask ourselves is, do options traders make any money? That was one of the questions explored in a 2022 study titled 'Losing is Optional: Retail Option Trading and Earnings Announcement Volatility' written by de Tim de Silva and others.[5] What they found was that most options trades made by small, individual investors took place before a particular company announced its quarterly earnings. Why would this be the case?

The primary factor that determines the price of a stock is the company's earnings. This makes perfect sense when you consider that when you buy stock in a company, you are buying ownership in the business and the value of that business is driven by the current and expected future profits of the business. If Nike's stock is trading at $100 per share, it's because investors have a certain belief about the company's future profitability. There are analysts that cover a company like Nike and come up with projections about how much money the company will make that year, which helps determine the current price of the stock. If Nike reports quarterly earnings that are lower than expected, the stock price will fall and vice versa.

Someone trading options on Nike is more likely to do so in anticipation of the quarterly earnings results. If they want to bet Nike's earnings will underperform market expectations, they buy a put option, and if they think Nike's earnings will be higher than expected, they buy a call option.

Put simply, options trading allows someone to make a bet on what's going to happen to the price of a stock in the near term. The research from de Silva found that when investors trade options in this way, they engage in 'a trio of wealth-depleting behaviors'.

1. *They overpaid for the options they bought.*
2. *They paid high transaction costs.*
3. *They were too slow to respond to changes in market prices.*

In other words, most people who trade options have no idea what they're doing. As a result, options traders were found to have lost between 5-9% when they used options to bet on the results of a company's quarterly earnings. For more volatile companies, the losses grew to 10-14%. If the most likely scenario from trading stock is that you lose money, then the most likely scenario from trading options is that you lose money - only you lose more of it, and you lose it quicker.

It's not just the finfluencers who want you to day trade

To buy and sell stocks, options, or index funds, most people use an online broker such as Robinhood. The economics of these online brokers differ from firm to firm, but they all have one thing in common: the more often you trade, the more money they make.

As I will cover in the next chapter, the best investing strategy for you is to buy a handful of low-cost index funds and sit on them for the next 40 years. Your broker does not want you to do that because they make next to no money if you do. What's best for your broker is that you make as many transactions as possible; the more often you buy and sell stocks, the more money they make. They make even more money if you trade options, regardless of what happens to your investment.

Insurance as an investment

I graduated from university with a Bachelor's degree in economics in 2010. This was the lowest point of the Global Financial Crisis of 2007–2008. The previous three years had brought the worst job market in nearly 100 years.

I was desperate for any job I could get my hands on so I took a job as a 'financial advisor' with an insurance company. But here's the thing about financial advisors who work for insurance companies: they might have the title of a financial advisor, but in reality most of them are little more than insurance sales people.

The product the bosses told us to sell to every client we talked to was whole life insurance. It's called 'whole life' insurance because the insurance cover stays with you until you die. This differs from 'term' life insurance, which provides you cover for a specified period—say 10 years—and then expires.

If you are wondering why we were encouraged to push whole life insurance over term coverage, it might have something to do with the fact that whole life insurance is much more expensive than term life insurance, which means more fees for the firm and more commissions for the sales reps. In fact, I was told that my first client should be myself and that I—a 22-year-old with no dependents—should open up a whole life insurance policy for myself. Yikes!

One of the strategies to sell whole life insurance to people who don't need it is to market it not as insurance, but as an investment: 'Okay, you may not need insurance right now, but you should start investing and building compound interest!' Yes, many of these whole life insurance policies have an investing component baked into the product. Here's a brief explanation of how they work. Whole (or permanent) life insurance policies have what's called a cash value, which you can think of as a savings account inside your policy. You can choose to have the insurance company invest those savings to further increase your cash value.

It's important to know that what the person selling you life insurance often fails to tell you is that most of these benefits are not unique to life insurance. You can get similar benefits without paying the high fees and commissions associated with life insurance.

- *Tax-deferred growth: the investment gains inside an insurance policy grow on a tax-deferred basis. That means you don't need to pay any taxes on your investment gains until you withdraw the funds in the future. If that sounds familiar, it's because that's how retirement savings plans work in every country that has one. Except, most retirement savings accounts have lower fees and commissions, meaning you get to keep more of your money.*

- *Borrowing against your cash value: insurance salespeople often argue that you can receive 'tax-free income' by borrowing against the cash value inside your insurance policy. But they might downplay the fact that doing so will reduce the death benefit your beneficiaries would receive, which defeats the entire point of life insurance.*

It's not uncommon for someone selling whole life insurance to receive a commission equal to one year's worth of premiums the day you sign on the dotted line. The insurance company is the one writing the check to the salesperson, but you, the policyholder, pay for that commission through increased fees baked into your monthly premium payment.

The thing you need to always remember about life insurance is that even if it has an investment component, it is, first and foremost, an insurance policy. That's easy to forget when it's pitched as an investment, but remember that you are signing a contract with the insurance company: you keep paying the premium, and they keep providing coverage.

Ultimately, investing inside a whole life insurance policy is expensive and complex. Investments and insurance serve different purposes in your financial life, so the vast majority of people will be much better off if they buy cheap term life insurance and invest in the stock market while minimizing their investment fees, which is what we will discuss in the next chapter.

How to invest in the stock market

I f you want to be a great investor, all you need to do is embrace this simple instruction: diversify, buy and never sell.

Put all the other garbage about investing that you hear from finfluencers out of your mind. You do not need to study company balance sheets, understand what a candlestick chart is, or what a P/E ratio stands for. Most people who tell you that these things are necessary to be a successful investor only have a surface-level understanding of them themselves. So say it with me again: diversify, buy and never sell. The best way to achieve this is to invest in low-cost index funds.

What is an index fund?

Index funds replicate an index of assets like stocks or bonds. For example, an S&P 500 index fund replicates the S&P 500 index, a list of the 500 largest companies in the US. If you own an S&P 500 index fund and the S&P goes up 2%, your index fund would also go up 2%.

Index investors do not buy a stock; they buy the entire stock market. The fund passively mirrors what happens in the entire stock market. This means as long as you hold on to an index fund, your investment returns will be equal to the average return in the stock market minus the investment fees, which for index funds are negligible.

"The beauty of diversification is it's about as close as you can get to a free lunch in investing."

- *Barry Ritholtz, Co-founder of Ritholtz Wealth Management*

What does a diversified portfolio actually look like?

I want to pull my hair out when I read about an investing guru's 'diversified portfolio', only to find out that their idea of diversification is owning 10 overvalued tech stocks that they are sure will be the 'future winners'. A truly diversified investment portfolio has three crucial elements:

1. *Investing in different types of assets*
2. *Investing in assets in different geographical locations*
3. *Buying all the assets in each asset class in which you invest*

It's crucial to understand why it's important to diversify a portfolio in the first place. Diversification has two benefits:

1. *It eliminates unnecessary risk, which is risk that does not add to your expected investment returns*
2. *It reduces your portfolio's volatility, making it easier to stay invested when the stock market hits a rough patch*

Put simply: proper diversification can maximize your odds of achieving your investment goals.

Diversifying by buying different types of assets

The two primary assets in most investment portfolios are stocks and bonds. Stocks are likely to be the primary asset class in your portfolio, with bonds playing a supportive role in reducing volatility and providing income. That's why one of the most popular ways to construct a portfolio is the 60/40 portfolio, which is made up of 60% stocks and 40% bonds.

For bonds to be an effective diversifying asset, they should have a low correlation, meaning they don't always move in the same direction as stocks. Critically, bonds should maintain a low correlation during downturns in the stock market.

So, what is the track record for bonds as an effective way to diversify a portfolio anchored by stocks? Here's some useful data from US-based investment advisor Vanguard highlighting the returns and volatility of portfolios that range from 100% bonds to 100% stocks from 1926–2020.[1]

	Average return	Negative return	Worst year
100% bonds	6.1%	1 year in every 5	1969 (8.1% loss)
20% stocks/80% bonds	7.2%	1 year in every 6	1931 (10.1% loss)
40% stocks/60% bonds	8.2%	1 year in every 5	1931 (18.4% loss)
60% stocks/40% bonds	8.6%	1 year in every 4.3	1931 (26.6% loss)
80% stocks/20% bonds	9.8%	1 year in every 4	1931 (34.9% loss)
100% stocks	10.3%	1 year in every 3.8	1931 (43.1% loss)

Here are a few lessons we can learn from these model portfolios.

- *If your only goal is to maximize annual investment returns, a portfolio of 100% stocks is rational.*
- *However, a portfolio of 100% stocks is incredibly volatile, and few investors have the stomach to stay invested in a portfolio that aggressive over several decades.*
- *Adding bonds to a portfolio will likely reduce your annual return but will also make the investment ride a whole lot smoother.*

That last point is very important because it highlights an inescapable truth about investing: if you want higher investment returns, you need to take on more risk. But to be a successful investor, you can't just look for the portfolio with the highest returns on paper. You need a portfolio that maximizes your returns while not being so risky that you panic and sell at the worst possible time. If adding bonds to your portfolio allows you to stay invested for 40 years rather than four, then sacrificing a little bit of annual return is a great deal.

Diversifying by geography

This is the part of diversification that people struggle with the most. Even investors who agree it's important to diversify their portfolio often fail to diversify by geography, which means investing in assets outside of your home country. Wherever you live, you likely have a bias towards investing your money within that country.

This home country bias is especially understandable for US investors. From 2010–2020 the US stock market outperformed international stocks by 8% per year. Except there is no reason to believe that outperformance will continue. Historically, the performance of US vs international stocks has been a pendulum; in one ten-year period international stocks have outperformed, and in another, US stocks have outperformed. According to a 2020 research paper by Vanguard, there's a decent chance that the pendulum will swing back in favor of international stocks before too long.[2]

To understand why international stocks may be due for a comeback, it's important to understand what factors contributed to the outperformance of US stocks in the 2010s and early 2020s. The largest factor was rising valuations for US companies compared to non-US companies. Rising valuations mean that investors have to pay more for every dollar of profit a business generates. You need to remember that by investing in stocks, you are not buying a piece of paper. You are buying partial ownership in a real business. The initial valuation when you buy a stock significantly impacts your expected return as an investor. All else being equal, buying at historically high valuations implies lower expected returns and vice versa.

Remember that US stocks outperformed non-US stocks by 8% per year during the 2010s. According to Vanguard's research, 68% of that outperformance was attributed to the expanding valuations of US stocks. If the valuations of US stocks don't continue to rise in the 2020s, there is little reason to believe the same level of US outperformance will continue.

Another key factor is the dominance of the US dollar relative to other currencies. After the financial crisis, the US economy rebounded faster and stronger relative to most other countries, which led to a demand for US dollars and an increase in the value of the dollar. A rising dollar means that assets held in other currencies are worth less than an asset held in US dollars. If the dollar continues to rise, that will contribute to a possible scenario of continued US outperformance. If the dollar weakens, that will contribute to international stocks outperforming US stocks.

Vanguard expects international stocks to outperform US stocks through the year 2030. Of course, this is just one estimate. Nobody knows for sure what the future holds for US or non-US stocks, which is exactly why you diversify by investing within and outside your home country.

Buy everything

Earlier I mentioned that to increase investment returns, you need to take on more risk. That is only partially true. To really increase investment returns, you need to take on more risk that you are compensated for taking.

Some investments decisions—like buying individual stocks—add to your risk but don't add to your expected returns. To explain why this is, you need to understand a few technical terms, don't worry, I'll make this part as simple and painless as possible.

- *Systematic risk = the risk that the entire stock market will go down. Whether you invest in the entire stock market or one just stock, you are exposed to systematic risk.*
- *Risk premium = the difference in returns between risky assets like stocks and risk-free assets like short-term government bonds.*
- *Idiosyncratic risk = the risk that is unique to an individual stock or sector. For example, if you invest in an oil company, a risk that's unique to your investment would be the world accelerating its timeline to stop using fossil fuels.*

The only reason you take on the risk of investing in stocks is that you are rewarded with higher expected returns via the risk premium. The risk premium compensates you for taking on risk. Investing in an individual stock does not give you a larger risk premium but it does add to your investment risk. Idiosyncratic risk can be diversified away with index funds so that you only take risks for which you are compensated.

The rational investor seeks to maximize expected returns without taking more risk than necessary. Since index funds mirror the entire stock market, investing in them literally means 'to buy everything'.

The 1% difference and the importance of minimizing investment fees

Diversification by buying different types of assets in different countries is not an exclusive feature of index funds. Actively managed investment funds—funds that pay an investment manager to pick and choose stocks and other assets—can also provide similar levels of diversification. So, you might ask, does it matter if I buy actively managed investment funds instead of index funds?

Yes, it does matter. Index funds are a superior investment for two reasons. First, by overweighting particular stocks or particular sectors, an actively managed investment fund exposes you to idiosyncratic (aka uncompensated) risk. Second, actively managed investment funds charge much higher fees than investment funds.

The most effective description of why active funds underperform index funds that I have ever read comes from a 1991 paper written by William Sharpe.[3] Here's the key quote from the paper: 'Before costs, the return on the average actively managed dollar will be equal to the return on the average passively managed dollar.' Remember, passively managed index funds replicate the entire market so it will provide investors the average market return before costs. If you add up every stock picker and investment fund manager, they will, on average, return the same as the market average before costs. Put another way, if you were to pick an actively managed investment fund at random, we would expect it to have the same returns as an index fund before investment costs are accounted for. This leads us to the inescapable truth that fees are the most important factor to consider when choosing an investment.

Index funds and actively managed funds both charge an annual fee for investing your money. Index funds don't have to pay a big-shot Wall Street stock picker to run the fund, so the fees you pay are a fraction of what you'll pay for an actively managed investment fund.

The annual fee for actively managed funds in the US typically ranges from 0.5-2% per year. If you had $10,000 invested, you would expect to pay between $50 and $200 per year in fees. By contrast, at the time I write this, Vanguard's S&P 500 index fund has an expense ratio of 0.03%. If you had $10,000 invested in the S&P 500 index fund, you would pay $3 per year in fees. Let's consider a hypothetical where you are presented with two investment options.

- *Option 1 is an index fund that tracks the entire global stock market and charges you an annual fee of 0.1%.*
- *Option 2 is an actively managed fund that picks stocks from around the world and charges you an annual fee of 1.1%.*

We'll assume that both funds provide an annual rate of return of 8% (although of course, this is impossible to know in advance). Since both funds provide global diversification with the same annual returns, the only difference is the fees, with the active fund having 1% higher annual fees than the index fund. After accounting for fees, the index fund has a net return of 7.9% per year, while the active fund has a net return of 6.9% per year. If you started with nothing and invested $500 per month for 40 years, you would have $1,695,778 if you invested in the index fund and $1,276,125 if you invested in the active fund. That's a difference of $419,653, or 28% less wealth, purely as a result of paying an additional 1% more per year to have someone pick stock for you rather than investing in index funds.

Jack Bogle's investment revolution

Fintech companies and crypto bros love to describe the new investment products they are peddling as a way to 'democratize' investing or as an investment 'revolution'. But here's the thing: investing has already been democratized. Today, nearly everyone can invest in the stock market for virtually no fees by investing in index funds. The investment revolution is over, and we won.

The leader of this investment revolution, whom National Public Radio famously referred to as 'the George Washington of investing', was the founder of Vanguard, Jack Bogle. Vanguard and Bogle did not create the first index fund, but they brought index investing to the mainstream.

Before Bogle founded Vanguard in 1974, the world of investing was dominated by stockbrokers who could get away with charging enormous fees for picking stocks on their client's behalf. The lie that Wall Street wants you to believe is that you need their investment advisors to manage your money for you. That's how they got away with charging such high fees in a futile effort to 'beat the market'.

Bogle understood an essential truth about the stock market, which is that it is one of the few arenas in life where the harder you try, the worse you will do. The more you try and beat the market, the lower your returns are likely to be. Bogle understood what few did at that time: the sensible investing strategy is to buy the whole stock market and minimize the fees you pay along the way.

At the time I write this, passively managed index funds account for approximately 16% of money invested in the US stock market compared to only 14% held by actively managed funds. The investment revolution is over, and passive index funds have won the day. As a result, it has never been simpler, faster, or cheaper for middle-class workers to invest in the stock market and secure their family's financial future.

So, the next time you log into your investment account and buy the entire stock market for fees that are next to nothing, give thanks to the investment revolutionary Jack Bogle who made it possible.

'Don't look for the needle in the haystack. Just buy the haystack!'

Jack Bogle, founder of Vanguard

Three different paths

Now it's time to learn how to put the theory into practice. This chapter will review the three paths you can take to build and manage an investment portfolio.

Path #1: Pure DIY investing

To be a successful Do It Yourself (DIY) investor, you must check three boxes.

1. *You have a clear understanding of the theory and logic behind investing in index funds.*
2. *You have the financial capacity and psychological fortitude to hold on to your investments for several decades without selling.*
3. *You feel confident in your ability to construct and maintain a portfolio.*

In Chapters 4 and 5, we explored in detail the theory behind investing in index funds and why it's likely to provide superior results to the alternatives like stock picking and high-cost, actively managed investment funds. It's essential for any long-term investor. In Chapter 3, you learned how to manage your finances to minimize the odds of being forced to sell your portfolio due to financial hardship. Part 2 of this book will be dedicated entirely to helping you build the investor mindset and psychological resilience required to stay invested even during recessions and market crashes.

We have yet to discuss that third box you need to check off as a DIY investor: how to construct and maintain a portfolio of index funds. This is one of the least discussed but most important aspects of managing your own investments.

How to construct a portfolio as a DIY investor

I need to introduce another financial term vital for any DIY investor to understand, and that is 'Exchange Traded Fund', or, as I'll refer to them going forward, ETFs. An ETF is an investment fund that can be bought and sold on stock exchanges in the same way as individual stocks. If you are a DIY investor using an online brokerage, you will almost certainly invest in index funds using an ETF.

Many new investors don't realize that index funds and ETFs are not the same thing. Index funds are defined by their passive investment strategy of replicating a particular index of assets. ETFs are defined as a specific structure of an investment fund. Not all index funds are ETFs, and not all ETFs are index funds.

Now that we have the basic terminology down, the next question many new investors have is what to look for when deciding which ETF index fund to invest in. There are hundreds of index ETFs to choose from, many of which look identical but have subtle important differences. Here are three important factors to consider when deciding which index ETFs to buy.

Factor 1: Management Expense Ratio (MER)

An index fund has one job: replicate the performance of a particular index. For example, an S&P 500 index fund is designed to replicate the performance of the S&P 500. That is the job of all S&P 500 index funds.

If all index funds have the same job of tracking a particular index, then the silliest thing you can do is to pay more than you have to for an index fund. That is where Management Expense Ratios (MERs) come into play. An MER is a fee you pay to the fund which pays for all the costs of running the fund. MERs are a percentage of the money you have invested in the fund.

Let's assume the other two factors I'm about to discuss are equal, and you are left with deciding between two S&P 500 index funds. One fund has an MER of 0.20% and one has an MER of 0.02%. Which should you choose?

This is not a trick question, although it might feel like one. We have been conditioned to believe that you 'get what you pay for' in life and that low cost is synonymous with low quality. Investing is the exception to this rule. Paying more in fees does not lead to a better investment outcome; in fact the truth is the opposite: the lower the fees, the better your investment outcome is likely to be. When it comes to investment fees, you get what you don't pay for.

Since these index funds do the exact same thing, the only rational choice would be to pick the fund with lower fees. Why would you pay one penny more than you have to when deciding between two virtually identical products? Whatever type of index fund you're considering investing in, the first thing you should look for is the MER of the various funds that track the same index.

Factor 2: Commission
This has less to do with the ETF you want to buy and more to do with which online broker you buy the ETF from. Some online brokerages charge a commission every time you buy an ETF. These fees are often around $5 or more per transaction. That means if you spent $100 buying ETFs, you

could be charged $5 for that transaction. This can seriously eat into your returns over time. For that reason, before you start your DIY investing journey, you should take your time to find the right online broker that allows you to buy ETFs for the lowest price possible.

Factor 3: Tracking error

An index fund has one job: mirror the performance of the index it tracks. The tracking error is the difference between the index fund's performance and the performance of the index it seeks to track, measuring how good an index fund is at doing its one job.

Returning to the example of an S&P 500, the tracking error tells us how closely the index fund mirrors the performance of the S&P 500. If the S&P 500 returned 10% in a given year and my S&P 500 index fund had a 9% return, the tracking error would be 1%. Index ETFs with the lowest tracking error will give you the most reliable results.

How to rebalance a portfolio as a DIY investor

Once you have created a portfolio of index ETFs, your work isn't done; you still need to rebalance your portfolio periodically, to ensure you maintain the asset allocation on which you based your investment plan.

Rebalancing is like pruning your hedges; if one area gets too overgrown, you need to trim it back. If you decide on a target for a 60/40 allocation of stocks and bonds, what will happen is that over time, your actual portfolio allocation will drift away from that target. If the stock market outperforms, you might end up with a 70/30 allocation, which is more aggressive than you had planned for. Rebalancing would involve selling off some stocks and buying some bonds to return to your 60/40 target allocation.

So how often should you rebalance your portfolio? There is no correct answer to this question; what matters is that you choose a rebalancing strategy that you'll be able to stick with. You could decide to rebalance based on certain dates every year. For example, if you decided to rebalance once a year, you might choose to do this on an easy-to-remember date like 1 January. Alternatively, you could set a rule that you rebalance whenever your asset allocation strays too far from your target. For example, if your target allocation was 60/40, you could decide that as soon as your allocation moves 10% off your target—to either a 70/30 or 50/50—you reallocate back to your target.

The more ETFs you have, the more complicated it will be to track and rebalance your portfolio. Many DIY investors get carried away and end up buying as many as ten or more ETFs to reach their target allocation between stocks and bonds and domestic versus international assets. Buying too many ETFs creates a major (and avoidable) headache when it's time to rebalance your portfolio.

For DIY investors, simplicity is your friend. If you are a financial minimalist, you can even invest in a single index ETF that offers a fully diversified portfolio in a single fund. For example, you can invest in a balanced fund ETF that holds a pre-determined asset allocation, like a 60/40, and takes care of the rebalancing for you. With a balanced fund, the only decision you need to make is how much money to invest each month. You'll likely pay a higher MER for a balanced fund, but if the idea of maintaining and rebalancing a portfolio either intimidates or bores you, the simplicity and time saved may be well worth it.

DIY investing is the lowest cost approach, but it is not for everyone. So, if the idea of managing your investments is giving you a panic attack, that's perfectly fine; it just means you need a little help. Let's discuss the two other options or paths available to you to get some help building and managing your portfolio.

Path #2: Using a robo-advisor

A robo-advisor is a digital investment platform. Using algorithms, it automatically manages your investments according to your goals.

After answering a series of questions and inputting your financial information, the robo-advisor will use an algorithm to suggest a diversified portfolio based on your risk preferences, goals, and individual circumstances.

Robo-advisors typically cost a fraction of what a traditional financial planner costs and can help someone with no investing experience construct a diversified portfolio in a single day. As with human advisors, it's important to do your homework and research different robo-advisors to find the one that fits your circumstances.

If you do decide to use a robo-advisor, it's important that you pay attention to what's being recommended. Don't forget you are the one in charge. If the robo-advisor recommends a 60/40 allocation and you're in your twenties, have a solid financial foundation, and have a high risk tolerance, you may want something a bit more aggressive.

When choosing a robo-advisor, you'll want to compare the fees each one charges. Some robo-advisors charge as little as 0.25% in fees, which works out to $25 per year for every $10,000 you have invested. (Note that this fee is in addition to the MER of the funds in which the robo-advisor invests your money.)

You'll also want to do your homework to ensure that the robo-advisor follows a passive, low-cost indexing strategy. Remember that robo-advisors are a business; like any business, their primary goal is to maximize profits. Some robo-advisors have learned that a low-cost portfolio is good for the investor but can be a lousy business, unless you are Vanguard with trillions of assets under management.

In recent years, some robo-advisors have pivoted to offer actively managed portfolios and included exotic (expensive) assets like crypto in their portfolio. This allows them to charge higher fees, which is a better business model but isn't in the investor's best interest.

Picking a robo-advisor with reasonable fees that follows a passive index strategy is a perfectly viable path to investing success.

Path #3: Hiring a financial advisor

If you don't want to manage your investments on your own and you want help from an actual human being, you may consider hiring a financial advisor. Hiring a financial advisor is a big financial decision that should not be taken lightly. If you are considering this route, here are eight questions you should ask them.

Question 1: Are you a fiduciary?

If a financial advisor is a fiduciary, this means that they are required to recommend investments that are in your best interest. If an advisor is a non-fiduciary, they only need to recommend an investment that is suitable for you. That gives non-fiduciaries the green light to recommend investments that will pay them big commissions, even if it's not what's in your best interest. So, ask the question and if the answer is anything but yes, end the meeting.

Question 2: What is your investment philosophy?

In Chapter 5, I presented the evidence as to why investing in low-cost index funds is an optional strategy for long-term investors. After reading that chapter, you might assume that the majority of financial advisors agree and will invest their client's money in index funds. That would be a dangerous assumption. The sad reality is that many financial advisors still recommend their clients invest in high-cost, actively managed mutual funds and other high-fee alternatives to index funds.

Why do advisors still recommend high-cost investment products despite the growing evidence that low-cost, passive investment strategies outperform? Each advisor would have their own explanation, but I am reminded of a quote from Upton Sinclair (see overleaf).

Question 3: How do you get paid?

Financial advisors typically get paid in one of two ways.

1. *Charging a percentage of the investments they manage, aka the 'Assets Under Management' or AUM model.*
2. *Charging an hourly or flat-rate dollar amount, aka the 'fee-only' model.*

For Gen-Z and millennials who aren't already wealthy, advisors working under an AUM model may not want to work with you. Under the AUM model, financial advisors don't get paid directly by their clients; instead, they take a percentage of the investments they manage on behalf of their clients. It's not uncommon for advisors to charge 1–2% of the value of your investments each year.

Say you have $500,000 in retirement savings that a financial advisor is managing on your behalf. If the advisor charges a 2% annual fee, they will

'It is difficult to get a man to understand something when his salary depends on his not understanding it.'

Upton Sinclair, writer and political activist

make $10,000 each year. If you only have $5,000 to invest, there is no financial incentive for a financial advisor to even speak to you, unless they want to sell you expensive whole life insurance that you don't need.

Under the fee-only or 'fee or service' model, advisors charge per hour, per job, or on a monthly subscription fee. This model works much better for young professionals who might be earning a solid income but have not yet had time to accumulate a significant amount of investable assets.

Question 4: What kind of asset allocation would you use for me?

Asking this question will reveal how the advisor approaches diversification. Will they have you in a mix of stocks and bonds? Do they believe in international diversification? How aggressive or conservative will the portfolio be? The advisor should be crystal clear on all of these issues.

Question 5: What services do I get for the fees I pay?

Financial advisors offer a wide range of services beyond portfolio management, ranging from insurance to estate planning. Asking what services are included with their fee is an opportunity for you to negotiate a tailored financial plan that only includes services you need or want at this time. Don't pay a higher fee for services you aren't going to use.

Question 6: What credentials do you have?

Financial advisors often have a long, confusing list of different credentials and designations that read like a bowl of alphabet soup.

The two most widely respected credentials on the financial advice space are:
- *The Certified Financial Planner (CFP)*
- *Chartered Financial Analyst (CFA)*

As a rule of thumb, you will want to work with an advisor with one of these credentials.

Question 7: How often will we meet or speak?

It's important to have a clear expectation of how often your advisor will be in contact. Will it be once per year? Every quarter? Or will you have unlimited access to speak with them if you need to ask a question? You'll also want to be clear if on when the advisor will charge you additional fees for additional meetings, especially if you are working with a fee-only advisor.

Question 8: If I work with you, are there any additional fees that we have not discussed yet?

In addition to the advisor fees, what are the fees of the investments they will put you in? If you decide to end your relationship with the advisor, will they charge you a fee or penalty? Before you sign on the dotted line, ensure you know your all-in costs if you decide to hire the advisor.

Whichever option you choose, remember you are not locked in for life with that option. If you don't have the time or confidence to manage your own investments today, you might consider hiring a human or robo-advisor. But nothing is stopping you from firing the advisor and managing your own money if and when you feel comfortable doing it. Working with an advisor is a life choice, not a life sentence.

Whether you decide to become a DIY investor, use a robo-advisor or hire a human financial advisor, it's critical you do your homework in advance and pick the option that suits where you are at in your financial journey right now.

Win as a long-term investor

Once you have built a portfolio of low-cost index funds, 99% of what you need to know to be a successful investor is expertly summarized by Warren Buffett: "Time is your friend: impulse is your enemy. Take advantage of compound interest, and don't be captivated by the siren song of the market."

Let's start with a simplified formula for compound interest: **A= P(1+r)^t**

where:

A= How much money you end up with
P= The amount of money you invest
r= The annual return your money earns while invested
t= The number of years your money is invested

This is the part where I am supposed to ask you to rank these variables in order of their importance. Except that's the wrong question. They are all important. The useful exercise is to rank these variables based on the level of control you have over each. Here's the correct ranking.

#1 – Number of years your money invested
#2 – The amount of money you invest
#3 – Annual return your money earns while invested

The siren call of getting rich quick

If you get most of your information about investing online, then you may be under the delusion that your annual return on investment is both the most important investment variable and that you can control it, which as we have already covered, it's not and you can't.

A surprisingly dangerous time in your financial life is the first year after you've started investing. It's at this point that a frustrating reality kicks in: building an investment portfolio is simple, but sticking with your plan and building wealth slowly for years—or even decades—is hard.

After a year of adding money to your portfolio on every payday, you may feel like you have made little progress, and you might start to feel frustrated. 'Why is this taking so long?!' New investors are like those people who sign up for a gym membership, go to three sessions with the personal trainer, and then wonder where their six-pack is.

If your expectation is that the stock market is some kind of elevator to wealth and financial freedom, you'll become very susceptible to the idea of a wealth-building shortcut and engage with finfluencers who want to sell you their 'stock market secrets'. The truth is that there is no shortcut, and the stock market does not come with an elevator; you're going to have to take the stairs. Investing in low-cost index funds is a slow path to wealth, but it's also the most reliable path.

Time in the market is more important than timing the market

The variable that investors have the most control over is how long they stay invested. Sadly, many investors sacrifice time invested (something they can control) in a futile effort to maximize returns (something they can't control).

"Time is your friend; impulse is your enemy. Take advantage of compound interest, and don't be captivated by the siren song of the market"

- Warren Buffett,
CEO of Berkshire Hathaway

'The most important thing is to stay the course - not to get shaken out of the market during a difficult time'

John W. Rogers, Jr, Co-CEO of Ariel Capital Management

Most people's greatest investing-related fear is a market crash like the one in 2008 after the US housing bubble burst. If you are an index investor, a market crash is not the biggest risk to your wealth; you are. The easiest way to lose money as an index investor is timing the market.

Market timing is a strategy where investors move in and out of the market to avoid losses and buy in at the bottom after the market crashes. Investors who time the market believe that they know what is about to happen in the stock market. Anyone who believes that is delusional, because no one can really know what the future holds. But we have all heard the term 'buy low and sell high' so often that people think that to be a good investor you need to buy and sell to avoid getting wiped out by a market crash.

Buy low and sell high makes for a good bumper sticker but is terrible investment advice. In fact, most people who think they will buy low and sell high end up doing the opposite.

Investing during a recession

If you are young and have invested in index funds, what happens in the stock market today, even if it's a 2008-style crash, is nothing but noise. Volatility is painful and depending on what's causing the volatility—like a pandemic or a financial crisis—it can be downright scary. Enduring this pain and volatility in the short run is the price we must pay for the immense profits of investing in the long run.

A common situation where investors make fear-driven decisions that they later regret is when the economy is in recession. Never forget that the stock market is not the economy. I repeat, THE STOCK MARKET IS NOT THE ECONOMY!

They do not move in lockstep, and oftentimes, they move in opposite directions. It's not unheard of for the stock market to have some of its best days when the economy is having some of its worst.

The best explanation for this is that **economic data is backward-looking** while **stock prices are forward-looking**. When economists publish statistics about the current unemployment or GDP levels, they use data that is weeks or even months old; stock prices reflect the market's expectation of a company's future earnings.

When awful economic data gets released that shows millions of people lost their jobs, it's not uncommon for the stock market to be surging upwards. What's happening in the stock market today is a reflection of where investors think things are going in the future. If it was expected that the unemployment rate was going to jump and investors think the economy has bottomed out, they would start to buy more stocks, and prices would rise. Here's the problem: most people aren't thinking about any of this when they are watching their portfolio go down the toilet. They believe the stock market is going to get a lot worse, so they try to sell before that happens. On the opposite page is a timeline of events that might cause an investor to let fear manage their portfolio during times of economic uncertainty.

The sad irony is that for long-term index investors, even a market crash as severe and prolonged as the 2008 financial crisis amounts to little more than a speed bump on the road to building wealth. I am reminded of the wisdom of legendary investor Peter Lynch (see page 75).

The stock market crashes.

↓

Investors get scared and sell at the bottom, turning paper losses into real losses.

↓

They then sit on the sidelines and watch as the stock market recovers.

↓

Since the stock market (forward-looking) often recovers before the economy (backward-looking), they miss out on some of the best months to be invested in the stock market.

↓

Once the economy feels more stable, they think it is 'safe' to get back into the stock market, and they buy when prices are high.

↓

In short, they sell low and buy high, which is the exact recipe to have lousy investment returns.

For long-term investors, stock market crashes are a fantastic wealth-building opportunity. The saying 'What goes up, must go down' is often used to scare investors into believing that a stock market crash is just around the corner. While it's important to understand that stock market crashes are an unavoidable reality for long-term investors, an equally important—but under-discussed—reality is that 'what comes down, must go up'.

A 2017 paper written by William Goetzmann and Dasol Kim asks the question what happens after a crash?[1] Goetzmann and Kim studied stock market crashes from over 100 stock markets around the world from the years 1692–2015. In the data, they observed over 1,000 stock market crashes—which they define as a decline greater than 50% in a single year—and found two clear patterns.

1. *Stock prices tended to increase dramatically following crashes*
2. *Investors reduced their allocation to stocks*

Time and again, investors panic sell after the market crashes, which is of course the worst possible time to sell. Investors who engage in this kind of panic selling face double the pain: they sell right after some of the worst days in stock market history and they sit on the sidelines and miss out on some of the best days in stock market history.

Research from Merrill Lynch shows just how important it is to stay invested because of the disproportionate amount of lifetime wealth you will accumulate in the stock market in a very small number of days.[2] They examined the return on a $1,000 investment in the S&P 500 from 1989–2018 under three scenarios.

- *Scenario 1: The investor implements a buy-and-hold strategy.*
- *Scenario 2: The investor pulls their money out of the market and misses the 10 best-performing months.*
- *Scenario 3: The investor pulls their money out of the market and misses the 20 best-performing months.*

If you've been paying attention, you can guess that the buy-and-hold investor outperformed, but by how much might shock you.

- *The buy-and-hold investor turned $1,000 into $17,306.*
- *The investor who missed the 10 best-performing months ended with $6,959.*
- *The investor who missed the 20 best-performing months ended with $3,328.*

'Far more money has been lost
by investors trying to anticipate
corrections than lost in the
corrections themselves'

Peter Lynch, writer and former manager of
Magellan Fund and Fidelity Investments

Volatility works both ways; there are very bad days, but there are also very good days, where the stock market goes through the roof. The risk of market timing is that you pull your money out, expecting the market to drop, then it soars upwards, and you miss out on those gains.

The harder you try to be a 'good investor' and gain superior returns by timing the market, the more likely you are to lose money. The longer you stay invested, the better your odds of success. Luckily, how long you stay invested is only up to one person: you.

Want to build wealth faster? Increase your savings rate

There is a way to speed up the wealth-building process, but it is not accomplished by trying to increase your investment returns, it's accomplished by focusing on the variable that investors have the second most control of: how much money you invest.

First, let's construct a shared understanding of what it means to be wealthy. The traditional way of tracking wealth is to use your net worth calculation which simply equals all your assets minus all your debts. The problem is that this measure of wealth does not take your cost of living into consideration. $1 million is enough to make someone who spends $30,000 per year wealthy, but not someone who spends $300,000 per year. Being wealthy means having a lot of money relative to your living expenses.

Wealth should not be measured in dollars and cents but in time. As an investor, you should ask yourself this: how many years you could maintain your lifestyle if you never earned another paycheck for the rest of your life? The higher this number is, the wealthier you are.

If you adopt this measure of wealth, then the most important metric to monitor in your financial life is your savings rate, the percentage of your income you are saving and investing. The higher your savings rate today, the more wealth you will have relative to your expenses in the future.

There are two levers you can pull to increase your savings rate: cut your expenses, or increase your income. There are lots of personal finance tactics you can deploy to pull either or both of these savings levers: budgeting, cutting your biggest costs (usually housing), or picking up a side hustle. These are all effective tactics to save more money—but only if you follow through on them.

If I were to tell you to cut your housing costs in half or start a side hustle to save more money, you might agree with the idea, but you would likely find putting this into practice very difficult. Moving house and increasing the number of hours you work in a day will dramatically change your day-to-day reality. People are resistant to change, especially when it comes to big changes such as where they live. That is why so few people follow through on personal finance tactics that could dramatically impact their savings rate.

Allow me to suggest an alternative approach to increasing your savings rate that anyone can follow through on. Here are seven words that can change the trajectory of your financial life: **treat new money like it doesn't exist.**

If you just got a promotion that will clear an extra $500 per month, set up an automatic transfer of $500 from your checking account to your investing account every payday. Next year, you get a cost-of-living adjustment that nets you an extra $50 per paycheck: call up your bank and bump up your automatic savings by $50.

You may have heard of the term 'lifestyle inflation', which refers to the phenomenon where the amount of money you spend rises as your income increases, making it impossible to build a high savings rate. The impacts of lifestyle inflation are subtle and seem harmless at first, but left unchecked can kill your odds of reaching financial independence, because you'll need more and more money to maintain your lifestyle.

Saving the majority of every pay raise is what I call 'reverse lifestyle inflation'. The essence of this is to redirect any new money that comes your way into savings and investments. Let's dive into some examples of how reverse lifestyle inflation works and how it can help you increase your savings rate and build wealth.

First, I'll create some hypothetical numbers so that I can illustrate the power of reverse lifestyle inflation:

- *You make $50,000*
- *You currently save $0 per year*
- *You get a 3% annual raise*
- *You save 100% of your annual raise*
- *Your savings/investments earn a 5% annual return*

Now, let's run through some scenarios where you can use that new money to build wealth.

What to do when you get a pay raise

If you redirect your annual 3% raise to saving and investing, you can go from a 0% savings rate to a 26% savings rate in 10 years. By year 30, you would be saving nearly 60% of your income.

Your increasing savings rate combined with compounding returns eventually adds up to a serious investment portfolio. After 10 years, you'd have $105,000. After 30 years, you'd have more than $1.5 million. That is potentially a life-changing amount of money without having to drastically change your lifestyle. You will need to make adjustments to your lifestyle, but they are so small and gradual that almost everyone could begin following through right now.

These calculations look promising, but there are even more opportunities to boost your savings rate. Let's review two more scenarios where you can treat new money like it doesn't exist.

What to do when you pay off a loan

If you're in debt and have a plan to pay it off, I have some good news: you are in a prime position to practice reverse lifestyle inflation.

If you pay $350 per month on a student loan for 10 years, your spending habits adapt to the fact that you can't spend that $350 per month. The day you pay off the student loan is a fantastic opportunity to embrace reverse lifestyle inflation. Rather than absorbing that $350 payment into your budget, treat that money like it does not exist and redirect it to saving and investing.

If you redirect pay raises and the amount you used to spend on debt repayment, you can supercharge your savings rate and build wealth much faster. Let's add a few more numbers to our previous example.

- You have a $250 monthly credit card payment that will be paid off in three years.

- *You have a $100 monthly payment to a line of credit that will be paid off in four years.*
- *You have a $350 monthly student loan payment that will be paid off in six years.*

If you continue redirecting your annual raises to investing and invest your previous monthly payment once each loan is paid off, after 10 years, you'd have a 35% savings rate and a $191,000 portfolio. After 30 years, you'd be saving two-thirds of your income and have a $2.4 million portfolio.

What to do when money falls in your lap

Let's discuss one more scenario where new money comes your way, and that's when you receive a sudden financial windfall. This could be expected, like when your year-end bonus comes in, or unexpected, like when your rich uncle dies and leaves you an inheritance.

Let's continue this exercise and assume you redirect all your pay raises and former debt payments to investing but add in the assumption that 12 years into this process, your rich uncle dies and leaves you $30,000, which you immediately invest.

After 30 years, you would have over $2.5 million, simply by treating this new money like it doesn't exist and redirecting it to a portfolio of low-cost index funds.

Reverse lifestyle inflation in real life

The best financial advice is what you will actually follow through on. Is it realistic to expect you never to spend any salary raises or financial windfalls for the rest of your working life? Of course not. What I presented here was an extreme, oversimplified example. In this example, you would have saved

100% of your new income, which you almost certainly won't be able to do – at least not for too long.

What you need to do is adjust the concept of reverse lifestyle inflation and create a rules-based system. The rules should have you saving aggressively early on as you build up your savings rate and then relaxing once you hit certain thresholds.

Here's an example of a rules-based system to practice reverse lifestyle inflation.

- *Save 100% of new money until you reach a 10% savings rate.*
- *Save 75% of new money until you reach a 25% savings rate.*
- *Save 50% of new money after you clear a 25% savings rate until you are financially independent - then celebrate!*

New money is easier to save than old money. Redirecting a portion of that new money to a investments will make your financial life easier over time. Eventually, you'll put yourself in a position where a bit of good luck, like a promotion or an inheritance, can meaningfully change your financial life.

There's only one way you can influence your annual investment returns

While you can't control your investment returns, you can influence your expected returns by choosing how aggressive your portfolio allocation is. The more of your portfolio that's invested in risky assets like stocks, the higher your expected returns will be. A portfolio of 100% stocks will have higher expected returns than a portfolio of 100% bonds. So, yes, you can influence your returns, but that is done at the beginning when you select your portfolio allocation.

Here's a word of caution on selecting an extremely aggressive portfolio allocation like 100% stocks. While the stock market is likely to outperform the bond market over the long run, the ride will be very bumpy. If you can't handle the volatility of a 100% stock portfolio, you are unlikely to be able to stay invested long enough to capture the wealth-building gains you need to reach financial independence.

Morningstar produces an annual report titled 'Mind the Gap,' which measures the gap between the returns of ETFs and the actual returns that investors who buy those ETFs experience.[3] From 2011–2021 investors in ETFs earned 9.3% per year, even though the ETFs themselves earned nearly 11% per year during that time. The 1.7% gap is the cost to investors who either tried to time the market (and failed) or could not handle the volatility of the ETF they invested in and sold early, leaving money on the table.

It's not the return of what you invest in that matters, it's the return you are able to capture by *staying* invested. If that means giving up some expected returns in exchange for a level of volatility you can stomach, then so be it.

You'll never be Warren Buffett, and that's okay

Warren Buffett is one of the most famous investors of all time. His fame is due not only to his legendary performance as an investor but also to his investing advice, which has resonated with millions of people. For decades people have made the pilgrimage to Omaha to hear Buffett speak at the annual Berkshire Hathaway shareholder meeting. Many of these people invested in Buffett's company just for the privilege to attend the annual shareholder meeting, and hear Buffett speak in person.

'My wealth has come from a combination of living in America, some lucky genes, and compound interest'

Warren Buffett, CEO of Berkshire Hathaway

We can learn a lot from the wisdom of Warren Buffett. However, most people seem to have learned the wrong lessons. They hear Warren Buffett talk about how he picks stocks, and they try to emulate his success - which we know by now is a fool's errand.

When asked to describe his investment philosophy, Buffett once said: 'All there is to investing is picking good stocks at good times and staying with them as long as they remain good companies.' That sounds easy, and to Warren Buffett, maybe it is. But the odds of you picking stocks like Warren Buffett are similar to the odds of you shooting a basketball like Steph Curry.

Don't believe me? Even Warren Buffett does not want you to try and pick stocks like Warren Buffett. In Vanguard founder Jack Bogle's book, *The Little Book of Common Sense Investing*, Buffett is quoted as saying the following: 'A low-cost index fund is the most sensible equity investment for the great majority of investors . . . By periodically investing in an index fund, the know-nothing investor can actually outperform most investment professionals.'[1]

If we can learn one thing from Warren Buffett's investing success, it's to start early and stay invested for life.

Warren Buffett reportedly bought his first stock at 11 years old in 1941. That means he has been investing in the stock market for more than 80 years. If in 1941 you started investing $100 per month in the S&P 500, reinvesting any dividends you received, you would have $31,034,762 by 2022. That's more money than you would ever need.

Most of us won't have an 80-year time horizon, but the point is that even a small amount of money can add up to huge sums over a lifetime, as long as we stay invested long enough to take advantage of compound interest.

Part Two

The Mindset

Your brain is your enemy

Here is one of the best pieces of investing advice you'll ever hear: 'Make sure your worst enemy is not living between your own two ears.'

You might think that quote came from Warren Buffett, Jack Bogle, or another legendary investor. But you would be wrong. That quote came from surfer Laird Hamilton. When he said that, he was referring to managing fear while riding a big wave on his surfboard. But Hamilton's advice applies just as much to managing a portfolio as it does to managing a wave.

To be a successful long-term investor, you must realize that your worst enemy does live between your ears. You are human, which means that you suffer from irrational patterns of thought that can lead to some very poor investment decisions. But don't worry, you're not alone; these patterns of irrational thinking, or 'cognitive biases', as psychologists refer to them, impact every person on the planet. I can't stress this point enough: acknowledging that you are prone to bouts of irrational thinking does not make you 'stupid', 'weak', or 'broken'; it makes you human.

In this chapter, we will review some of the most common cognitive biases investors must deal with. The first step to adopting the long-term investor's mindset is to be aware of the irrational thought patterns that are most likely to push you off track.

To be clear, our goal is not to 'fix' these biases. The human brain is not like an old computer you can make work by unplugging it and then plugging it back in. The goal is for you to gain awareness of these biases so they don't dominate your decision-making. By the end of this chapter, you will better understand how the human brain interprets risk and how you can apply these lessons to better manage your portfolio in the long run.

Confirmation bias is the death of wisdom

'Exposure to a mixed body of evidence made both sides even more convinced of the fundamental soundness of their original beliefs. Confirmation bias is profoundly human, and it is appalling. When new information leads to an increase in ignorance, it is the opposite of learning, the death of wisdom.' —Will Storr, *The Unpersuadables*.[1]

Most people think confirmation bias is the tendency to seek out information that backs up what you already believe. The more accurate definition of confirmation bias reveals how insidious it truly is; confirmation bias is the tendency to interpret any new information as confirmation of your pre-existing belief. The difference is subtle but important.

Let's say you held the belief that Bitcoin is the future of money and that, in 10 years, it will become the dominant currency in the world. Confirmation bias is not just that you would look for articles and videos made by other Bitcoin enthusiaststst. If this was a strongly held belief, I could hand you a 50-page document outlining the pros and cons of Bitcoin, and you'd be much more likely to focus on the pros as evidence that you were right all along and you'd find a way to dismiss, minimize, or downplay the cons – even if there were more cons than pros. Acknowledging that you (yes, you!) have a tendency to interpret new information in a way that reinforces what you already believe is half the battle. The best investors are the ones who seek different viewpoints before making important decisions that impact their portfolios.

Loss aversion means hating to lose more than you love to win

If you go to a casino and lay down $20 on the roulette table, you will experience much more intense pain if you lose your $20 compared to the intensity of the joy you would feel if you doubled your money.

It's an unfortunate evolutionary trait that humans hate losing more than they love winning. It makes perfect sense that our brains have evolved this way when you think of how terrifying the world was for early humans. In the days when 'losing' likely meant getting eaten by a predator, the early humans who overreacted to the possibility of loss were the ones most likely to survive, reproduce, and pass along their genes.

While loss aversion is helpful when trying to stay alive, it might be the single most damaging psychological trait an investor can possess. Loss aversion is even more damaging because people are also prone to mental accounting, a term coined by famed behavioral economist Richard Thaler. [2]

Mental accounting describes the internal mental process of assigning different values to different pots of money. Rather than having one ETF that holds 60% stocks and 40% bonds, most investors would prefer to have two ETFs, one that holds stocks and one that holds bonds, and weigh them accordingly. In terms of our net investment returns, doing this adds no value and introduces unnecessary complexity. Even though it's irrational, most people like the idea of separating their 'risky' investments from their 'safe' investments.

So, what happens when you combine loss aversion with mental accounting? You get a myopic investor.[3] A myopic investor is someone who constantly checks their portfolio balance and feels anxiety every time they see their investments are down.

Even on days when the stock market closes higher than it opened, there will be many points throughout the day where the stock market is down; that's the nature of a volatile asset where prices are updated every few seconds. The more often you check your portfolio balance, the more times you will see the value going down—even if it goes right back up after you stop looking. Myopic investors hold on to the negative feelings when they see their portfolio going down and forget about all the times they checked and saw their portfolio going up. Your brain wants you to believe that you are constantly losing money.

The more anxiety and pain you feel from investing in volatile assets like stocks, the less likely you will be to stay invested. Myopic investors invest less in risky assets, and since it's risky assets that have the highest long-run returns, myopic investors build less wealth over their lifetime.

The solution to avoid becoming a myopic investor is simple: do not check the value of your portfolio. The only time you should be looking at your portfolio is when you have made a new deposit into your account and need to invest that cash, or when you need to rebalance your portfolio, which only needs to be done a handful of times each year. Another helpful tip to reduce your investing anxiety is to delete the stock market apps from your phone and never tune into financial media that focuses on the daily activities in the stock market. Out of sight, out of mind.

'If owning stocks is a long-term project for you, following their changes constantly is a very, very bad idea. It's the worst possible thing you can do because people are so sensitive to short-term losses. If you count your money every day, you'll be miserable'

Daniel Kahneman, psychologist and economist

Overconfidence is the path to underperformance

Arrogance, cockiness, hubris, ego, overconfidence – we have many different names to describe the ways that most people overestimate their skill and ability. Everyone believes they hold above-average ability – which is a statistical impossibility.

It's easy to think of ways overconfidence can damage your portfolio. Imagine you are a decade into your investing journey, and you've enjoyed a lot of success; your portfolio has done well, and each year you've been able to invest more money than you did the previous year. Slowly but surely, you forget that your success was due to following a simple strategy of buying index funds and taking what the market gives you.

If you start believing in your own hype, you might begin to believe that your incredible skills as an investor and superior knowledge of financial markets have led to your new-found wealth. So, you decide to take a more active role in managing your portfolio. Often, taking an active role in your portfolio means trying to time the market. We know by now that market timing is the easiest way for an investor to lose money. In Chapter 7, I pointed to research that showed investors underperformed the actual performance of the investment funds they owned by 1.7% per year. This happens from failed attempts to time the market. If an investor buys and holds an investment fund, they will have the same annual returns of that fund.

Think of this 1.7% annual underperformance as a tax levied against your portfolio for being overconfident. This can have devastating impacts on your ability to build wealth. If 1.7% does not sound like a lot, consider this: if you started from scratch, investing $500 per month for 30 years, here's how much 1.7% could cost you.

- *If you bought and held and earned 6% annual returns after 30 years, you would have $502,257.*
- *If you timed the market and, as a result, only earned 4.3% annual returns on the same investment, after 30 years, you would have $366,198.*

Your overconfidence 'tax' ended up costing you $136,059. Falling victim to overconfidence robs your future self of significant wealth while punishing your current self with increased stress and more time spent managing your investments. That is lost time that could have been spent making more money to invest, relaxing, or spending time with your loved ones. Therefore, the overconfidence tax not only costs you money but a much more precious resource: time. For investors, overconfidence is the path to underperformance.

The Dunning-Kruger Effect

'The first rule of the Dunning-Kruger club is you don't know you're a member of the Dunning-Kruger club.' — David Dunning, Professor of Psychology, University of Michigan

The Dunning-Kruger effect is named after it's creators David Dunning a professor of psychology at University of Michigan and Justin Kruger a professor at New York University Stern School of Business. The Dunning-Kruger effect describes the phenomenon where people with the lowest level of skill or knowledge grossly overestimate their abilities.

The original paper where Dunning and Kruger first describe this phenomenon is appropriately titled 'Unskilled and Unaware of It: How Difficulties in Recognizing One's Own Incompetence Lead to Inflated Self-Assessments.'[4] Dunning and Kruger had participants in their studies take tests measuring things like grammar and logic and then asked them to estimate what percentile they thought they would land in for each skill.

What they found was an inverse relationship between skill and perceived ability. Those who scored in the 12th percentile estimated themselves to be in the 62nd percentile. As test scores increased, participants did a much better job of assessing their own abilities. Those in the top 25% of test scores actually underestimated their own perceived skills.

Dunning and Kruger's explanation is that when we are truly awful at a particular task, we don't know enough about it to accurately assess our abilities or have any baseline for what expertise in this area would look like. I can't help but think of all the finfluencers who popped up during the pandemic telling their followers how easy it is to trade stocks and make money in crypto. Yes, some of these people were straight-up scammers. However, many were simply overconfident as well as ignorant of the realities of the stock market, so they overestimated their ability to trade stocks and teach others to do the same.

The Dunning-Kruger effect further highlights the danger of overconfidence. Those most at risk of suffering from overconfidence are the least likely to realize it, which makes it incredibly difficult to guard against.

If there's a bright spot in all of this, it's that Dunning and Kruger's research found that the more skill and knowledge someone had, the more accurate they became at forecasting their own abilities. What I take from this is that the more we dedicate ourselves to learning, the more we realize how much we don't know, which is a humbling experience. This is important for investors because it takes a lot of humility to say, 'I don't know what's going to happen in the stock market. Therefore, I will buy the whole market using an index fund and call it a day.'

I am reminded of this quote credited to Albert Einstein: 'The more I learn, the more I realize how much I don't know.'

Present bias keeps us from thinking long term

Present bias refers to the tendency for people to prefer receiving a smaller reward right now than waiting and receiving a larger reward in the future. Present bias causes us to think in the short run rather than the long run.

In a 1999 paper titled 'Doing It Now or Later,' Ted O'Donoghue and Matthew Rabin examine present bias and what they describe as 'time-inconsistent behavior', which is when someone makes a decision today that will negatively impact their future.[5]

As I pointed out in Chapter 2, when introducing the concept of financial time travel, I told you that investing by definition means thinking in the long run. If you suffer from present bias, you might find yourself asking why it's worth investing $500 per month for retirement when you could be enjoying that money today.

Short-term thinkers are also more likely to get scared by volatility in the stock market. If you spend too much time worrying about what happens in

"You know, some people say life is short and that you could get hit by a bus at any moment and that you have to live each day like it's your last. Bullshit. Life is long. You're probably not going to get hit by a bus. And you're going to have to live with the choices you make for the next fifty years"

- *Chris Rock*

the stock market today, it's easy to lose perspective and forget reassuring facts, such as no investor in history has ever lost money buying an S&P 500 index fund, reinvesting the dividends, and sitting on it for 20+ years. Investing is a form of self-care, but not for your current self. It's about caring about your future self.

The framing effect

Let's pretend there's a lottery that gives you a 50% chance of winning $1 million and a 50% of winning nothing. Which sales pitch would make you more likely to buy a ticket?

1. *Enter for a 50% chance of winning $0.*
2. *Enter for a 50% chance of winning $1 million.*

Clearly, you would choose option two. This is an extreme example of how the framing effect works. Both options accurately describe the lottery odds, but when certain features (possibly winning $1 million) are highlighted over other features (possibly winning $0) our brains are nudged into taking action—that's the framing effect.

You encounter much more subtle versions of the framing effect every day, even if you don't know it. Consider how disinfectant spray is typically marketed. The label would say something like 'kills 99% of germs'. You'd be much less likely to buy the disinfectant spray if the label said, 'only leaves 1% of germs alive.' The framing effect seems harmless when used in low stakes purchases, but remember what's happening with the framing effect; you are deciding based on how the information is presented, not the information itself.

'Seek instant gratification, or the elusive promise of it, and chances are you'll find a crowd there ahead of you'

Jeff Bezos, founder of Amazon

Every Ponzi scheme in human history has used the framing effect to make a scam look more favorable than legitimate investment alternatives. A Ponzi scheme is an investment scam where the scammer promises investors higher returns and less risk than traditional investment options. Ponzi schemes are named after famous con artist Charles Ponzi, who in 1920 offered investors the 'opportunity' to invest in his arbitrage scheme of buying discounted postage stamps in foreign countries and redeeming them in the US – a process he claimed would net a 400% return after costs.[6] He promised investors a guaranteed return of 50% within 45 days and that investors would double their money in 90 days. Talk about framing! While there was nothing illegal about this arbitrage process, the problem was that he was not actually buying and selling postal stamps. Instead, he would use money from new investors to pay out earlier investors who wanted to pull their money out. In August of 1920, *The Boston Post* ran an investigative piece exposing Ponzi's scam, and he was arrested shortly after.

The common consensus is that Michael Jordan is the greatest basketball player of all time. So, it is a fun bit of trivia that the silhouette of the basketball player on the NBA logo is not Michael Jordan but Jerry West. Charles Ponzi may be the Jerry West of Ponzi schemes, but the Michael Jordan of Ponzi schemes is the man who carried out the biggest Ponzi scheme of all time, Bernie Madoff.

Bernie Madoff and the Ponzi scheme

In 2008 Bernie Madoff was arrested for running a Ponzi Scheme that conned thousands of investors out of $65 billion over nearly twenty years.

Ponzi Schemes that offer ludicrous returns typically collapse in on themselves quickly. Ponzi's scam lasted less than a year because he promised enormous returns. 50% in 45 days and doubling your money in 90 days? That is going to draw the attention of investigators pretty quickly. Bernie Madoff's Ponzi Scheme went undetected for so long for two reasons.

1. *Unlike Charles Ponzi, Bernie Madoff did not promise ludicrous returns, like doubling your money in 90 days. What he promised investors was solid returns (15 - 18% per year) but with less risk than investing in an index fund.*
2. *Before his crimes came to light, Bernie Madoff had a spotless reputation in the financial services industry and even served as the chair of the Nasdaq multiple times in the early nineties.*

Madoff leveraged his reputation, connections to wealthy investors, and technical (some might say boring) investing strategy to frame how his victims would view the 'investing opportunity' he pitched to them. They invested with Madoff because they believed their money was safe. The investing strategy he pitched was a lie: he did not invest their money but used the money received by new clients to pay out earlier clients, much in the same way Charles Ponzi did. The house of cards collapsed in on itself during the financial crisis in 2008 when new money stopped coming in, and existing investors started pulling money out.

The easiest way to safeguard yourself against bad actors using the framing effect to lure you into an investment scam is to educate yourself about the basics of investing and financial markets. Never forget that when it comes to investing, returns and risk are tied at the hip. The higher the expected returns of a particular investment, the more risk is involved in that investment. You cannot have higher returns without taking on more risk. If someone pitches you an investment 'opportunity' that promises outsized returns with minimal risk, turn around and run away as fast as you can. If it feels too good to be true, it probably is.

Oversimplification tendency and the use of 'rules of thumb'

People prefer simplicity over complexity. The problem is that we don't live in a simple world. Most situations are much murkier and shaded in gray. Rather than taking the time to think through the various factors that come into play with a complex problem, most people look for a mental shortcut to focus on a single factor that is easy to understand. What then happens is that they tune out all the other (potentially important) information.

This tendency to oversimplify complex problems leads many people to rely on heuristics (or rules of thumb) to make decisions. One complex problem that investors have to solve is the issue of asset allocation. How much money should you allocate to riskier assets like stocks versus safer assets like bonds? Proper asset allocation requires deep thought and evaluation of several variables, such as how correlated your income is to the stock market, how much cash you have on hand, and forecasting how you might respond if the stock market dropped by 40%.

Rather than tangle with these complex questions, many investors turn to a rule of thumb called 'the rule of 110' to determine how much of their portfolio to allocate to stocks and bonds. According to this rule, the amount of your portfolio you allocate to stocks should be equal to 110 minus your current age, with the remainder being invested in bonds.

Using the rule of 110, a 30-year-old would have a portfolio of 80% stocks and 20% bonds, while a 60-year-old person would have a portfolio of 50% stocks and 50% bonds.

Like with many oversimplifications and rules of thumb, there is a kernel of truth within the rule of 110, which is that younger investors can more easily take risks compared to older investors. If you are 35 years away from retirement, you have a long time to recover if the stock market goes into the tank. On the other hand, if you are in retirement and too much of your portfolio is in stocks, a market crash could be disastrous for your retirement plans.

Every rule of thumb makes a trade-off between simplicity and accuracy. Sometimes, that trade-off is tolerable, especially if simple modifications can be made to the rule of thumb to make it more useful. But the rule of 110 is too simplistic and only considers one factor: the investor's age. Determining your asset allocation is too important a decision to be determined simply by your age.

Rules of thumb can be useful for someone to begin learning about a complex topic like asset allocation. But never forget the essential truth about rules of thumb: they should be your starting point, never your ending point, to understand a complex problem.

The bandwagon effect, aka 'group think'

The bandwagon effect is when people take certain actions because they feel like 'everyone else is doing it' and have a serious case of Fear of Missing Out (FOMO). The bigger a trend gets, the more people jump on the bandwagon and follow along.

There are thousands of publicly traded companies in the world, but most stock traders focus on a tiny fraction of those companies. The most common reason someone trades stocks is because other people are doing it. It's become commonplace for traders to gather in online communities and quite literally decide how to invest as a group. We even have a name for the kind of stocks that get traded in this way: 'meme stocks'.

Sadly, our media ecosystem does an incredible job at perpetuating groupthink and FOMO by focusing their coverage on the one trader who made a killing trading popular stocks, ignoring the dozens of other traders who lost their shirts. Making investments based on what's driving the news is a fantastic way to lose money.

A 2021 research paper titled 'Internet Search, Fund Flows, and Fund Performance' studied the returns of investors who invested in what's popular.[7] The researchers used Google search volume to explore the connection between investment funds that were grabbing headlines and the future performance of those investments. If an investment fund saw a spike in Google searches, the researchers wanted to know how much money poured into the funds after that spike in traffic and how the fund performed. They found that individual investors were more likely to buy funds that generated online buzz. Unsurprisingly, these attention-driven investors had negative future returns. There's a reason basically every investment fund on earth is required to disclose that 'past returns are not indicative of future results'.

'For every complex problem,
there is an answer that is clear,
simple, and wrong'

H. L. Mencken, journalist and cultural critic

There's a term for when investors pile new money into an investment after it's done quite well. It's called return chasing, and it usually ends badly. Here's how return chasing often plays out.

- *A stock goes on a hot streak.*
- *This leads to more media attention and online buzz.*
- *New investors contract FOMO and want to jump on this rocket ship before it goes to the moon without them.*
- *After all that new money gets poured into the stock, its price continues to temporarily increase.*
- *Sooner or later, the reality sinks in that this stock has become grossly overvalued, and early adopters who hold large positions sell their shares at a huge gain.*
- *The price comes plummeting back to earth, and the most recent investors—the ones who were return chasing—get wiped out.*

If you are too excited about what you are investing in, it's probably a bad idea; what you choose to invest in should be boring and easy to understand.

The anchoring effect and avoiding snap decisions

You walk into a department store and see two white t-shirts. You check the price tag on the first shirt and see that it costs $1,000. Then you check the price tag on the second shirt and see that it only costs $200. Both shirts look similar in quality, so you think the $200 t-shirt is 'cheap', even though paying $200 for a t-shirt is insanity. That's the anchoring effect in action.

In their 1974 paper titled 'Judgment under Uncertainty: Heuristics and Biases', Amos Tversky and Daniel Kahneman define the anchoring effect as follows.[8]

'In many situations, people make estimates by starting from an initial value that is adjusted to yield the final answer. The initial value, or starting point, may be suggested by the formulation of the problem, or it may be the result of a partial computation. In either case, adjustments are typically insufficient. Different starting points yield different estimates, which are biased toward the initial values. We call this phenomenon anchoring.'

Translation: If presented with two options, you will (at least partially) judge the second option relative to the first option.

In our t-shirt example, you judged the $200 shirt as cheap relative to the first shirt which was $1,000, instead of asking yourself: 'Is this shirt worth $200?'

The anchoring effect is one of the biases that can lead an investor to try to time the market. When the stock market reaches new all-time highs, investors start to get nervous. 'Why would I buy stocks right now when they are so expensive? I'll wait for the next market crash and buy when things look cheaper.'

That, my friends, is anchoring; you're comparing the current price of stocks in relation to a previous price of stocks and using that comparison to delay investing your money.

If we look at the data, we can see that investing when the stock market is at an all-time high has been less risky than you might think. Since 1958 the S&P 500 has set a new all-time high 18 times per year on average.[9] When the stock market sets a new all-time high, it's much more likely to set another new all-time high rather than crash. Research from JP Morgan shows that if you had only invested on days when the stock market set an all-time high, you would have a better return than if you invested on randomly selected days.[10]

If you are nervous about putting money into the stock market at all-time highs, resist the urge to compare today's prices to yesterday's prices and ask yourself, is the price in the future likely to be higher or lower than it is today? Then let the data and your financial plan guide your decisions.

Hindsight bias can distort the present reality

'Hindsight is of little value in the decision-making process. It distorts our memory of events that occurred at the time of the decision so that the actual consequence seems to have been a 'foregone conclusion.' Thus, it may be difficult to learn from our mistakes.' —*Diane F. Halpern, psychologist*

You may have heard the term 'hindsight is 20/20', which means once an event has already happened, people have a tendency to rewrite history and make it seem like what happened was obviously going to happen, when in reality, very few people predicted the event ahead of time.

After the 2008 financial crisis, every pundit covering financial news had the same conclusion: 'we should have seen this coming'. Once we have the results, it's easy to work backward and cherry-pick the clues that a thing was going to happen and conclude how obvious it was. But here's the thing, vanishingly few people called the financial crisis before it happened. If it was so obvious, then why did so few people see it coming? Because it was not nearly as obvious as our 20/20 hindsight would have us believe.

As an investor, the real danger of hindsight bias is how it distorts your view of the future. Living through stock market crashes is so painful that it scars your memory and makes you think the next big crash is imminent.

But here's a comforting truth: stock market crashes like the one in 2008 are much less common than your hindsight bias would have you believe. Since 1929, the S&P 500 has seen eight stock market crashes where the market has dropped by 40% or more from its peak.[11] That works out to about once every 12 years. Even more comforting is that six of those eight stock market crashes happened before the Second World War. Since 1939 the stock market has only had two market crashes of 40% or more: once in 1973/1974 and then again in 2007/2008. History repeats itself, but not nearly as often as we think it does.

Familiarity bias and why you shouldn't invest in what you know

Legendary investor Peter Lynch once said, 'Buy what you know.' With all due respect to Mr Lynch, investing in 'what you know' plays into another well-documented cognitive bias, the 'familiarity bias', which is the natural tendency for people to prefer what they are already familiar with and avoid the unknown. But limiting your investment opportunities to what you already know can lead to disastrous results.

The most common version of investing in 'what you know' is buying the stock of the company you work for, which exposes you to unnecessary levels of risk. Consider an extreme example where 100% of your net worth is tied up in the stock of the company you work for, which also happens to provide you with 100% of your income. Then a series of scandals and fraud by upper management comes to light, the company goes bankrupt, and you are left quite literally with nothing. No assets and no income.

If you think that could never happen, consider the case of Enron, an energy company which was one of the largest companies in the United States. On 5 February 2001, the company's stock closed at $81.81; by the end of the year, it closed at 60 cents per share after it was revealed that the company was engaging in fraudulent accounting practices that made it seem like the company was making more than it was.

Here's the devastating part about the Enron story. When it declared bankruptcy in 2001, 60% of the assets in Enron employee retirement accounts were made up of Enron stock.[12] Enron employees invested in what they knew, and in the blink of an eye, they lost 100% of their income and 60% of their retirement savings.

You can avoid a similar fate by diversifying a portfolio. By definition, proper diversification means investing in all types of businesses, most of which you will know nothing about. Educating yourself about investing is important, but you should never let familiarity bias lead you into an avoidable trap where your investments and income come from the same source.

Self-serving bias

People have a rather toxic tendency to attribute their success to their own brilliance, until they fail, when they immediately look for some outside source, either a person or an event that happened in the world, on which to blame their failure: 'It's not my fault I lost our life savings in a meme stock. It's the corrupt Wall Street system conspiring against the little guy.' Psychologists call this inherent lack of accountability 'self-serving bias'.

Everyone looks like an investing genius during a bull market, when the price of just about everything is going up. A fatal mistake new investors make during bull markets is that their current investing success can be attributed to their brilliant investment choices. This can lead to serious overconfidence and lead to more reckless investment choices like picking individual stocks.

It's not until the bull market turns into a bear market (prices go down) that the consequences of poor investment decisions are revealed. As Warren Buffett once said: 'You don't find out who's been swimming naked until the tide goes out.' Except the self-serving bias can prevent the naked swimmers from noticing their nakedness.

Investors picking up the pieces after their reckless decisions blow up in their faces are likely to look for external factors to blame.

- *It's the crappy economy.*
- *It's the government's stupid policies.*
- *It's the central bank raising interest rates.*
- *My employer doesn't pay me enough, so I had no choice but to take these risks.*

Self-service bias keeps investors from accepting the hard truth: they are terrible at picking stocks and should never have attempted to do so in the first place. The same goes for market timing or any other overly complicated investing strategy.

If you've made it this far into this book, you already know the sensible way to invest your money: invest in a risk-appropriate portfolio of low-cost stock and bond index funds, and don't sell until you've hit your financial goals. If you deviate from the plan and get burned, accept the responsibility for that mistake but don't dwell on it—just get back to the original plan.

The investor's mindset

Every long-term investor needs to be aware of Hofstadter's Law, which states: 'It always takes longer than you expect, even when you take into account Hofstadter's Law.'

Douglas Hofstadter is a professor of Cognitive Science and Computer Science at Indiana University and won the Pulitzer Prize for general non-fiction in 1980 for his book *Gödel, Escher, Bach* where he coined the phrase "Hofstadter's law".

Hofstadter's Law encapsulates the true difficulty of building wealth: it takes longer than you would like, which leads to impatience, and the more impatient you get, the more susceptible you are to 'get rich quick' schemes and other shortcuts.

I would like to propose a new law called 'Le Fort's Law', which states: 'If the obvious solution to a problem is patience, there will always be charlatans trying to sell you a shortcut.'

The diet and fitness industry is a perfect example of Le Fort's Law. Losing weight is a slow process that involves a balanced diet and regular exercise over a prolonged period of time. But for decades supplement companies, trendy diets, and fad workout routines have all promised to help you lose weight in record time.

Building wealth is a slow process that involves regular contributions to a diversified portfolio over a period of several decades. Knowing that most people lack that kind of discipline and patience, charlatans are all too eager to offer their method of speeding up the process—for a fee, of course. The sad irony is that these shortcuts often blow up in investor's faces, which only serves to further slow things down.

While the wealth-building process is slow to get moving, once you hit a tipping point, compound interest starts doing the heavy lifting. Let's examine a hypothetical situation to show you what I'm talking about, based on the following assumptions:

- *You have a 40-year investment horizon.*
- *Every month, you invest $500.*
- *Your average annual return on your investment is 6%.*

If you followed that plan without market timing, panic selling, or falling for the siren calls of get-rich-quick schemes, after 40 years, you would have $1,312,406. But it's slow going in the early years; in fact, it would take 19 years before your total lifetime investment gains surpass your lifetime contributions. In the first half of your investing journey, you are doing all the heavy lifting to build wealth.

And after 19 years? This is when compound interest takes over, and building wealth becomes a breeze. In the first year following this plan, you would have invested $6,000 and earned $196 in returns. In year 40, you still would contribute $6,000 but would have enjoyed $88,256 in investment gains in a single year. That's the pot of gold at the end of the rainbow waiting for long-term investors.

The hardest thing you'll ever have to do as an investor is hang in there long enough to reach that tipping point where compound interest does the heavy lifting. In addition to the charlatans selling you modern-day snake oil in the form of wealth-building shortcuts, you'll need to battle against the cognitive biases we looked at in Chapter 8. To stay invested long enough to reap the benefits of compound interest, you must develop the investor's mindset, which focuses on rational optimism and resilience.

Why it pays to be an optimist

The simplest definition of optimism is having positive expectations about future events. Keep that simple definition in mind as we discuss how optimism impacts how you manage your portfolio.

Are optimists better at managing money and building wealth than pessimists? That was the central question of a 2007 paper by Manju Puri and David Robinson, who are both Professors of Finance at Duke University's Fuqua School of Business.[1] They asked people how long they expected to live, then compared their answers to the average life expectancy of someone of the same age, ethnicity, health status, and lifestyle. They defined an optimist as someone who expects to live longer than their actual life expectancy.

They also found that those who were optimistic about how long they would live were more optimistic about other aspects of life, including the future of the economy and their income. Even when controlling for past income growth, optimists held a strong belief that their income would grow significantly over the next five years. Optimists believe they will be around for a long time and that the future of the economy and their place in it is strong. These are all necessary beliefs for anyone who expects to keep their money invested for 30–40 years.

"Optimism is a strategy for making a better future. Because unless you believe that the future can be better, you are unlikely to step up and take responsibility for making it so"

- *Noam Chomsky, linguist*

Puri and Robinson tested how optimism impacts three major financial life decisions.

1. *Retirement planning*
2. *Career choices*
3. *Investing*

Optimists work harder and earn more money

To quote Puri and Robinson: 'We find that more optimistic people work longer hours, anticipate longer age-adjusted work careers, and are more likely to think they will never retire. Optimists work more in their younger years, and they work more than the average person does when they reach retirement age.

If you associate optimism with aggressive financial goals like early retirement, it might surprise you to learn that optimists work more even once they reach retirement age. Puri and Robinson theorize that optimists overestimate their 'marginal product of labor', which is an economist's way of saying that optimists overestimate the benefits of working more.

An optimist might typically approach their career by thinking 'If I respond to that email after hours, the bosses will be sure to notice and give me the promotion.' Even if they don't get the promotion, they will continue to work harder than pessimists.

Just because optimists overestimate the benefits of hard work doesn't mean that they don't have successful careers; they do. It means optimists work really freaking hard. This makes sense if you compare them to pessimists. Why would you bother working hard on your career if you did not believe you could be successful?

Remember, the only way to speed up the wealth-building process is to make more money so that you can invest more money. Optimists work harder, earn more lifetime earnings, and therefore have more money to invest.

Optimists save more money

The least surprising result in Puri and Robinson's work is that optimists save more money than the average person. Someone will only save money for their future if they expect to be around to enjoy the fruits of those savings.

The more surprising result was that optimists were more likely to pick stocks rather than diversify their portfolios through index funds. What's even odder is that optimists don't invest more of their money in the stock market – but with the money they do invest, they take unnecessary risks by picking stocks.

So if optimists work harder, save more money, and make irrational bets on individual stocks you might be left wondering whether optimism is a good thing or a bad thing as an investor. Puri and Robinson wondered the same thing, so they went deeper into the data and separated optimists into two groups.

1. *Moderate optimists, who we will call 'rational optimists'.*
2. *Extreme optimists, who we will call 'irrational optimists'.*

Irrational optimists were the people who scored in the 95% percentile for optimism; even by the standard of optimists, they are extreme outliers in their confidence about the future.

Which type of optimist should I be?

Rational optimists save the most money, pay their bills on time, are the least likely to fall into debt, plan their finances for the long run, work harder than any other group of people, and are much less likely to engage in reckless investing strategies like stock picking and day trading. The description of a rational optimist is the description of someone who has the best chance to stay invested for the long run.

Irrational optimists, on the other hand, are as bad as pessimists. They were less likely to think about their finances in the long run, more likely to fall victim to overconfidence and engage in overly risky investing strategies, and saved less money than rational optimists.

Optimism is essential, but too much of a good thing can be harmful to your wealth. You need to be optimistic to be a great investor, but you also need to think rationally and not fall into the trap of overconfidence.

The rational optimist strikes a balance between being confident in their future while not losing a grip of what is (and isn't) within their control.

Can optimism be learned?

If you consider yourself a pessimistic person, the first question you must ask is whether optimism can be learned later in life?

The question of whether optimism is inherent or learned was the central question of a 1992 paper titled 'Optimism, pessimism and mental health: A twin/adoption analysis'.[2] The researchers studied 500 pairs of fraternal twins, half of which were raised together and half of which were adopted apart as infants. Then they studied the level of optimism and pessimism in the twins that were raised together and the group adopted and raised apart and then measured how much of their optimism or pessimism is inherent, and how much is attributed to environmental and learned behavior. They found that optimism is 23% inheritable, while pessimism is 27% inheritable. This means that more than 75% of optimism comes from learned behavior rather than your inherent genetic make-up. That is tremendous news for anyone who wants to increase their level of optimism.

It's also important to know where your starting point is and what environmental factors have impacted your current level of optimism. A natural assumption might be that people who grew up with money are optimists, while people who grew up in households that struggled financially would be pessimists.

It turns out that it's not so simple. A 2009 paper titled 'Socioeconomic Disparities in Optimism and Pessimism' sought to answer that very question; does growing up rich make someone more optimistic, and growing up poor make someone more pessimistic?[3] The paper's authors found that growing up in a low-income household made someone more likely to be a pessimist but growing up in a high-income household wasn't any more likely to make someone an optimist. No wonder there are so many pessimists in the world.

Five exercises to increase your level of optimism

Here are five daily activities that have been linked to increased optimism.

1. Practice mindfulness
2. Count your blessings
3. Cleanse your social media timelines
4. Imagine the best possible version of your finances
5. Learn to challenge negative thoughts about investing

1. Practice mindfulness

If you are the type of person who rolls their eyes at the idea of practicing mindfulness, hear me out. The research suggests mindfulness is an effective way to cultivate a more optimistic mindset.

You might be wondering, what does 'mindfulness' even mean? The Mayo Clinic defined mindfulness as a 'type of meditation in which you focus on being intensely aware of what you're sensing and feeling in the moment, without interpretation or judgment.'[4]

One of the more interesting studies examining the link between mindfulness and optimism was a 2020 study titled 'Compassion meditation increases optimism towards a transgressor'.[5] The researchers wanted to know how a mindfulness practice would impact someone's level of optimism, even when they are tasked with writing a personal letter to a convicted murderer.

The participants in the study were split into two groups. Group one performed daily mindfulness practices for eight weeks before writing their letters, while the other group did not practice mindfulness. After the eight weeks, the group practicing mindfulness wrote more positive, optimistic letters than the control group because, to quote the paper, 'they valued positivity more.' If practicing mindfulness can make someone more optimistic about a convicted murderer, could it help you be more optimistic about your investments?

Here are some exercises from the Mayo Clinic to practice mindfulness, which I have altered slightly to keep the focus on your portfolio.[6]

Pay attention to how different aspects of investing make you feel

Next time you deposit money into your investment account, take a moment and notice how you feel. Does investing money make you feel excited, empowered, or anxious? Ask yourself what is making you feel the way you do at that moment.

When you think about your portfolio or financial future, notice how your body feels at that moment. What physical sensations do you feel in your body, and where in your body are you feeling it?

Don't place a judgment on your feelings

When you think about a decision you made that impacted your portfolio, try not to judge the situation as either inherently 'good' or 'bad'. It simply 'is'.

If you made a poor investment decision, like picking individual stocks, timing the market, or putting your money into a complex 'alternative' investment and it blew up in your face, try not to focus on how silly or costly that mistake was. Instead, focus on what you will do in the future. Remember worrying is only useful if it's related to something we have the power to change, and as you learned in Chapter 2, financial time travel only works to affect your future. You can't change the past!

Be kind to yourself

Most people are a lot harder on themselves than they are on their friends. If you make an investment mistake that costs you money, your inner dialogue might be along the lines of: 'how could I be so stupid?' But what if your best friend came to you and was beating themselves up over making the same mistake? Would you call your friend an idiot or show them compassion? Treat yourself the way you would treat your best friend.

Focus on your breathing

If you are feeling overwhelmed by negative thoughts or worries about your portfolio—say during a steep market crash—sit down, close your eyes, and take slow and controlled breaths for at least 60 seconds. Then open your eyes and remember that these types of unpleasant events are not out of the ordinary but are expected and unavoidable realities that all long-term investors must deal with. Remind yourself that this is the exact moment where you can guarantee your future success by simply doing nothing and waiting out the storm.

2. Count your blessings

A 2005 study documented the benefits of practicing gratitude; in their research, the authors studied which mental exercises had the biggest impact on someone's happiness and level of optimism.[7]

One of the most effective interventions in the study was the 'three good things' exercise. Participants in the study were instructed to write down three good things that happened during their day, with emphasis on what caused that good thing to happen. After one week of repeating this exercise, participants in the study were less depressed, more optimistic, and happier than those in the control group. Focusing on good things that happen in your life and your role in those things happening cultivates optimism.

As a first actionable step towards adapting an optimistic mindset you can participate in the "three good things" exercise. Over the next week, write down three good things that happened in your financial life each day. Be sure to include what caused that good thing to happen and be especially mindful of when you were the cause of that good thing.

3. Cleanse your social media timelines

You've probably heard the term 'doom scrolling,' which is when someone constantly seeks out and engages with negative news on social media. Doom scrolling is one of the easiest ways to remain pessimistic about the future.

A 2021 study measured the impact of doom scrolling COVID-19-related news on people's mental health and levels of optimism.[8] The study consisted of two experiments; in the first experiment, participants were split into two groups. The first group was exposed to just two minutes of negative COVID-19-related news on Twitter and YouTube. The control group did not receive any news related to COVID-19.

In the second experiment, participants were once again split into two groups. The first group was shown positive COVID-19-related news that highlighted random acts of kindness and how communities and families rallied together to support each other during the worst of the lockdowns.

The researchers found that consuming as little as two minutes of negative news on social media was enough to lower participants' well-being and optimism. They also found that consuming positive news on social media did not negatively impact someone's level of optimism about the future.

This tells us that social media is not inherently toxic; it depends on what kind of accounts show up in your timeline. If you find that your social media timelines are filled with toxic, negative posts, it's time to cleanse your timeline. The social media algorithms respond to what you engage with. Every time you engage with an account that peddles negative commentary, you send a message to the algorithm to serve you up more of the same.

'Be thankful for what you have; you'll end up having more. If you concentrate on what you don't have, you will never, ever have enough'

Oprah Winfrey, talk show host and producer

Don't engage; simply block every social media account that engages in negative messaging about financial issues. If someone writes something like 'PREPARE FOR THE BIGGEST MARKET CRASH OF THE CENTURY', block them, and you won't have to see their garbage ever again.

On the flip side, follow and engage with accounts that provide positive, nuanced, and evidence-based commentary. Over time your social media timeline will become less toxic, and you'll have less opportunity to fall victim to the optimism-crushing habit of doom scrolling.

4. Imagine the best possible version of your finances
A powerful exercise to cultivate optimism can be found in a 2010 paper titled 'Manipulating optimism: Can imagining a best possible self be used to increase positive future expectancies?'[9] Participants in the study were split into two separate groups.

- *The first group was asked to think about their best possible self for 1 minute.*
- *Then the first group was asked to write about a typical day in their best possible life for 15 minutes.*
- *The control group was asked to write about a typical day in their current life for 15 minutes.*
- *After 15 minutes of writing, both groups were asked to reflect on what they wrote for an additional 5 minutes.*

The researchers found that participants in the 'best possible self' group had increased expectations of positive events and decreased expectations about negative events in their future compared to the control group. I challenge you to find a better definition of optimism than that. Here's some good news for the pessimists out there. The results were not dependent upon a participant's initial level of optimism or pessimism; the exercise benefited 'natural' optimists and pessimists equally.

Here are some instructions to adapt the 'best possible self' exercise to your financial life.

1. *Start by setting a timer for 1 minute and spend that time imagining the best possible version of your financial life. Imagine yourself in the future after you have achieved every financial goal you have ever dreamed of. You have worked incredibly hard for years to achieve these goals, and you have finally done it. Think about what it would feel like to achieve all your financial goals and dream. This is your best possible financial future.*

2. *Next, set the timer for 15 minutes and start writing about a day in your life after achieving your best possible financial future. Don't worry about spelling or grammar: just keep writing until the timer goes off.*

3. *Finally, set the timer for 5 minutes. Imagine as vividly as possible everything you wrote about. Think about what a day in your life would look like once you have achieved your best possible financial future.*

5. Learn to challenge negative thoughts about investing

Let's conclude our discussion of optimism by laying out a framework that you can use to challenge negative thoughts that enter your mind and prevent negative thinking from pushing you towards destructive behavior.

A 2001 article written by Felice Miller published in the *Western Journal of Medicine* laid out the importance of challenging the negative thoughts we have about our behavior.[10] Once again, imagine that you have made a big investment mistake: you took the advice of a finfluencer and invested in a meme stock, it blew up in your face, and you lost $10,000. As Miller points out, people tend to subscribe to an unrealistic expectation that we must always make the right decision in every circumstance in life, including investing. If we hold ourselves to an impossible standard, failing to live up to those standards can lead us down a dark spiral of thinking.

- *It starts with an unrealistic assumption like 'I must always make perfect investment decisions to be successful'.*
- *You then make a bad decision, because you are human, and humans are prone to making bad decisions. But instead of acknowledging that it's okay to make mistakes, you think: 'I should never have bought that meme stock; I am such an idiot.'*
- *Negative thoughts begin to escalate and you start thinking, 'I will never be able to recover from this.'*
- *Those negative thoughts turn into feelings like shame, regret, and anger.*
- *Eventually, you manifest physical symptoms such as headaches or fatigue.*
- *This leads to poor behavior, such as avoidance or blaming yourself or others.*

Miller lays out several steps we can take to manage a stressful event, like losing $10,000 on a poor investment. Give this a try the next time you find yourself stressed over an investing mistake.

Before your thoughts begin spiraling out of control, write down and describe the situation you are in. Be sure to identify what you are thinking and feeling, any physical symptoms (like headache), and how your behavior might have changed.

Miller highlights that it's important to understand that it's your thoughts about yourself ("I must be perfect at all times") and not the stressful situation ("I lost money") that drives our thoughts, feelings, physical symptoms, and behavior changes. Ask yourself if your thoughts and feelings are realistic. Is it a realistic expectation that you should always make perfect investment decisions? Of course not. Even wealthy people and successful, long-term investors make mistakes.

Here's an example of how Miller would suggest you challenge negative assumptions and thought patterns around a stressful financial situation. Again, we will use the hypothetical situation of losing $10,000 betting on a meme stock that went bust. Start with a realistic assumption like 'I am not perfect, and everybody makes investing mistakes.'

Next, reframe how you perceive a mistake. In this example, you might think, 'I made a mistake and feel uncomfortable. I have lost some money, but this does not make me a financial failure.' Try to turn your feelings in a productive direction. Instead of feeling shame for having made a bad investment, feel determined that you will find more money to invest and avoid making the mistakes that led you here ever again.

As a result, the physical symptoms you are likely to feel are positive, such as increased focus and alertness. You will then be more likely to engage in positive behavior, such as re-examining your budget to find more money to invest or looking for more credible sources of information before making investment decisions in the future.

If you're going to commit to being a long-term investor, you must accept that you will make mistakes along the way. What will determine your success is how you respond to your mistakes.

Optimism breeds resiliency

The greatest benefit of cultivating an optimistic mindset is not all the warm and fuzzy feelings of positivity you imagine you might feel on a daily basis; instead it's that optimistic people are more likely to have a resilient mindset. Here's how the American Psychological Association defines emotional resilience: 'Resilience is the process and outcome of successfully adapting to difficult or challenging life experiences, especially through mental, emotional, and behavioral flexibility and adjustment to external and internal demands.'[11]

A bad thing happens; you adapt and make the best of it and move forward. Be warned: lifelong investors are going to experience a lot of 'bad things'. Recessions, depressions, pandemics, wars, political unrest, climate disasters, and financial crises are all things you can guarantee will deliver a body blow to your portfolio at one time or another if you plan on staying invested over the next 40+ years.

Resilience as an investor is being able to take the body blow that the world hits you with, get back up and keep moving forward with your plan as if nothing happened. Resilient people are not only less likely to panic during a stock market crash, but they are also more likely to see the crash for what it is; the wealth-building opportunity of a lifetime.

Researchers have found that optimistic people are much more likely to be emotionally resilient too.[12] If you believe the future holds good things for you, then you are much more likely to be able to pick yourself up and dust yourself off when bad things happen. If you don't believe that success is in your future, the first external event, like a recession, will hit you like a freight train.

Once you figure out how to build a portfolio, 90% of long-term investing —staying invested long enough for compound interest to work its magic—is about how you respond during bear markets and recessions. That's why every long-term investor needs to be emotionally resilient.

Change your internal narrative

One of the most self-destructive human tendencies is our ability to replay bad things that happen to us on an endlessly repeating loop in our heads. Psychologists refer to this tendency to relieve negative events as 'rumination'.

Few things can kill resilience like rumination. Research has shown that rumination can cause otherwise healthy people to feel depressed and anxious.[13] Breaking out of the vicious cycle of rumination is table stakes for anyone looking to build resilience and researchers have found that practicing mindfulness can help people break out of this cycle.[14] You'll remember that mindfulness was also helpful in cultivating optimism, which further clarifies the connection between optimism and resilience. Research on mindfulness in the context of rumination found that it is much more effective at breaking the cycle of rumination than trying to solve the problem.

This is doubly important for investors because when the stock market crashes, there is nothing you can do to 'fix' the problem. The only fix is to wait as long as it takes for the market to recover; leaping into action is the worst thing you can do after a stock market crash.

Take a page out of the stoic's playbook

'The chief task in life is simply this: to identify and separate matters so that I can say clearly to myself which are externals not under my control, and which have to do with the choices I actually control. Where then do I look for good and evil? Not to uncontrollable externals, but within myself to the choices that are my own.' — Epictetus

The philosophy of stoicism offers a lot of benefits to investors. Stoics strive to concern themselves only with things that they can control and understand that there is nothing to be gained by tying ourselves into knots over what we can't control, especially things that have already happened.

The more you worry, the more you pick away at your emotional resilience. Worrying about things that you can't control—like what happens in the stock market—will drain your resilience without providing any positive ROI.

If you're going to worry, make sure you worry about things you can actually control. You can't control the outcome, but you can control your process. You cannot influence whether the stock market goes up or down, but you can control how long you stay invested, how aggressive your portfolio is, if you have cash emergency funds available, and how much money you invest every month. You control the process.

If you can direct all your energy to the process of investing rather than the outcome, you'll have what it takes to be a long-term investor.

Financial habits for long-term investing

'Habit is the intersection of knowledge (what to do), skill (how to do), and desire (want to do)'

Stephen R. Covey, author of
The 7 Habits of Highly Effective People

That quote from Stephen Covey, author of *The 7 Habits of Highly Effective People*, is a useful overview of what you've learned in this book. In Part One you gained the knowledge required to be a successful investor, reviewing what to do and, crucially, what not to do when investing your money.

In Chapters 8 and 9 you learned the skills required to stay invested for the long run by confronting your inherent investing biases and using exercises to develop an optimistic and resilient mindset. In this chapter, we close the loop and talk about how to identify 'bad' financial habits and replace them with healthier ones that can help you accumulate much more wealth over your lifetime.

Identifying bad financial habits

A habit is simply a behavior or action that is regularly repeated. If habits are repeated often enough, you may not even be aware that you're doing them. This is useful because it allows us to complete tasks without dedicating any mental resources to work through the details.

Consider a simple act like walking up the stairs. How mentally drained would you feel at the end of the day if every time you had to walk up a flight of stairs, you had to stop and consider if you would lead with your left or right foot or what you would do once you reach the top of the stairs? Luckily, we have formed a powerful habit that allows us to walk up a staircase without giving it a second thought.

Habits tap into what Daniel Kahneman, author of the bestselling book Thinking Fast and Slow, would describe as our 'System 1' level of thinking, which is fast, intuitive, and emotional.[1] However, while forming habits to complete repetitive tasks is a useful evolutionary function of the human brain, it pays dividends to stop and evaluate some of the habits that are having a negative impact on our life.

Most people associate bad habits with addiction issues (smoking or drinking), diets (constantly snacking) or social media consumption (mindlessly doomscrolling), but most people have a few bad financial habits that need to be addressed as well.

How many times have you been waiting at the cash register in a grocery store and ended up throwing some trashy magazine or candy into your cart? You didn't enter the grocery store with the intention to drop an extra $25 on celebrity gossip and empty calories, but you did it anyway. This type of financial behavior is called impulse buying, a subtle habit that hits your bank balance. One survey found that US shoppers spent an average of $314 per month on impulse purchases in 2022.[2] Think of how much financial stress could be relieved if that money was redirected towards investments every month.

Impulse buys aren't the only bad financial habits you need to look out for. Constantly checking your portfolio is another nasty habit to which investors fall victim; seemingly unaware of the anxiety and poor decisions that stem from over-monitoring your investment performance.

Anything you do without thinking critically that harms your financial future is a bad habit.

Self-control is about planning ahead, not relying on willpower

One of the worst ways to go about breaking poor habits is to rely on willpower. How many diets have failed because the key to success relied on someone resisting temptation at every turn? Breaking any bad habit, whether it be dietary or financial, requires self-control but not willpower.

You might be thinking, aren't self-control and willpower the same thing? Nope. Willpower is reactive while self-control is proactive, which makes all the difference in the world. Before we delve into that idea, let's back up and ask two important questions.

1. *What does self-control even mean in the context of financial habits?*
2. *Will self-control help you spend less, invest more, and build wealth faster?*

A 2017 paper titled 'Does self-control predict financial behavior and financial well-being?' surveyed 2,000 people to measure if their financial behavior and financial well-being was linked to self-control, which they defined as 'our ability to break bad habits, resist temptations and overcome first impulses'.[3] They found that people with a high degree of self-control enjoyed a ton of financial benefits.

- *Saving more money*
- *Making better financial choices*
- *Feeling less anxious about money*
- *Feeling more secure about their financial situation.*

Reading that list of benefits, it sure sounds like self-control is pretty important if you want to live a richer, happier life with minimal anxiety. The question then becomes: how can you increase your level of self-control?
In 2021, researchers from Carleton University in Ottawa, Canada, published a study to pull together the research of financial self-control strategies across 29 academic studies to determine how effective they were at

helping people save more and spend less.[4] The researchers break down several different types of self-control strategies, but to simplify their findings, you can think of just two strategies to implement financial self-control and avoid falling to temptation.

1. *Proactive strategies*, which focus on what you can do to avoid tempting situations to overspend in the future.
2. *Reactive strategies*, which focus on what you can do to avoid overspending once you are in a tempting spending situation.

You won't be surprised to learn that proactive strategies were found to be much more effective than reactive strategies. Let's return to the example of dieting. A proactive strategy for eating healthily would be to avoid keeping any junk food in the house. By being proactive, or 'planning ahead', you reduce your reliance on willpower to avoid temptation and bad habits. If you keep junk food in your house, it's only a matter of time before it gets eaten. But if you get proactive and remove junk food from the equation, you won't have to rely on the myth that is willpower.

Let's apply this concept of proactive self-control to your financial life. Think about situations where you might be tempted to overspend and think of a strategy to avoid that ahead of time. Let's say a group of friends want to go out for dinner. This is a prime situation where you will be tempted to overspend. To avoid paying marked-up costs at a restaurant, maybe you offer to host a dinner party and ask each guest to bring an individual item. Someone brings a bottle of wine, another person brings dessert, and you cook the main course. You get the benefit of dinner with friends at a fraction of the retail cost. That's an example of a proactive strategy to practice financial self-control. Anticipate a situation where you will spend too much money and plan to avoid it.

We've discussed at length why constantly checking your portfolio balance is a destructive financial habit, as it increases the odds of making an emotionally driven decision that you will later regret.

The proactive strategy of self-control to avoid this habit is no different from the dieting strategy: remove the object of temptation from your day-to-day life. In the same way the dieter keeps junk food out of their house, you can keep easy access to your portfolio out of your phone. If you find yourself checking your portfolio balance too often, simply delete every app from your phone that would allow you to either view your portfolio balance or give you live updates of what's happening in the stock market. As they say, out of sight, out of mind.

Don't waste your time on 'millionaire habits'

One particularly cringe-inducing variety of influencer is the personal development guru. If you've ever spent significant time on LinkedIn, you will know exactly who I am talking about; the bros who want you to believe that the keys to untold wealth and career success come down to 'millionaire habits'. Some of the greatest hits on the list of these super habits include:

- *Waking up before the sun rises*
- *Reading at least one book per week*
- *Adhering to whatever new diet is trending that week*
- *Exercising early in the morning or late at night*
- *Ditching friends that don't meet your definition of 'success'.*

These posts are even more likely to go viral if they can attach these so-called millionaire habits to real-life millionaires – or better still, billionaires!

How many times have you read some variation of this headline 'The morning routine Elon Musk uses to propel him to success and how you can do the same.' This type of viral clickbait tends to have three key ingredients.

1. *Name-drops a well-known wealthy person to get you to stop scrolling.*
2. *Hints at the habits or routines that allegedly contribute to their success.*
3. *Strongly implies you can become ultra-wealthy if you click on the article.*

This is the height of influencer bullshit. Getting up at 4.30am is not going to make you wealthy. It won't even make you more productive – it will just make you really tired by the time you are halfway through your workday. I don't care how many Warren Buffett biographies you read while running on the treadmill at 4am before your ice-cold shower; if you make $3,500 per month and rent is $1,850; you aren't going to become a millionaire anytime soon.

Claims that adopting these types of habits will increase productivity are a distraction. Some of them might be helpful, others will be distinctly unhelpful, but none of them will make you wealthy. So by all means, get up at dawn and go for a run if you want to, but don't think that this is a guaranteed path to wealth

Actually useful financial habits

The first law of building wealth is that your income must be greater than your expenses. If you don't have extra money to invest at the end of each month, this needs to become your number one goal, because you're not going to build wealth until you have disposable income to invest. From there, the entire wealth-building process can be simplified into one sentence: continue to increase the gap between what comes in and what goes out and invest the difference.

Here are some 'habits' that can help you do just that.

- *Track your spending and cut the fat.*
- *Create a budget you'll stick to.*
- *Build an emergency fund.*
- *Pay off debt.*
- *Avoid lifestyle inflation.*
- *Build multiple streams of income.*
- *Invest through low-cost index funds.*

Then it's just a matter of consistency and patience. What you'll notice about all of these 'habits' is that they aren't really habits at all. They are individual components of a well-coordinated financial plan to build wealth. And the best part? None of these actions require you to live up to some impossible standard. If you can find a way to go from not investing at all to investing $100, then $500, and eventually $2,500 or more every month, it doesn't matter what time you get out of bed.

The way to break bad habits is to replace them with good ones

Once you've identified the bad financial habits you want to break and the good financial habits you want to implement, all that's left to do is swap out the bad habits for the good ones.[5]

In his New York Times bestselling book *The Power of Habit: Why We Do What We Do and How to Change*, author Charles Duhigg (overleaf) breaks down the science of how habits are formed and provides a blueprint for how you can replace your bad habits with good ones. Duhigg describes habit formation as a three-stage circular process.

1. ***Habits start with a cue.*** *The cue could be a time of day, a physical location, talking with certain people, or a news story you read or watch.*
1. ***That cue triggers a routine.*** *A routine is simply a pattern of behavior that your brain associates with the cue.*
3. ***At the end of the routine is the reward.*** *Your brain is stimulated by the outcome of the routine, which reinforces the routine the next time you notice a similar cue. Receiving a reward is what makes habits so powerful. Your brain begins to crave that reward, making the habit difficult to break.*

In this way, habits are a circular loop: cue, routine, and reward. Each time the loop repeats itself, the habit becomes stronger and more difficult to even notice, let alone break.

Let's say that as an investor you want to break the very destructive habit of constantly checking the balance of your portfolio. You need to start by diagnosing the habit and examining the three stages in this particular habit loop.

In this case, the cue might be getting a push-notification on your phone that the stock market dropped 5%. This triggers the routine, which is logging on to your brokerage account to see how much money you lost. The 'reward' is the illusion that by checking on your portfolio, you are taking control of your financial situation. Of course, this is irrational because you know that you can't control what happens in the stock market, and checking your portfolio only gives you more opportunity to make a fatal mistake like selling and locking in a loss. But that's the thing about habits; they tap into your System 1 level of thinking, which is fast, intuitive, and emotional; rational thinking has nothing to do with it.

Breaking any habit requires changing the routine that leads to the reward. In the example of checking your portfolio balance, the reward is the feeling of being in control of your finances. If what you want is to feel in control of your finances, switch out the 'bad routine' of checking your portfolio with a 'good routine' like tracking your spending.

The new habit loop might look something like this.

- *You receive a cue in the form of an article saying the stock market just dropped 5%.*
- *Your new routine is to track your spending over the past month and analyze which expenses you could cut to save and invest more money.*
- *The reward is the feeling that you are taking control of your financial situation.*

By identifying the three stages of the habit loop, you were able to replace the destructive financial habit of checking your portfolio balance in stressful situations with tracking and analyzing your expenses, a financial habit that will help you free up more money to invest and build wealth.

Building new financial habits and pulling a financial 180

If you need a powerful example of how replacing bad financial habits with good ones can change your finances and your life, look no further than Joel, creator of the popular blog 'Financial 180'.[6] Here's what I learned from Joel while listening to an interview where he described the impacts of financial habits on his life.[7]

When Joel and his wife graduated from college, they picked up high-paying jobs, which allowed them to finance some bad financial habits. They bought a single-family home in Florida in 2007 right before the market crash, had two cars, spent nearly $600 per month at large retail stores like BestBuy, ate out almost every day, paid for expensive food kit and water delivery services, and —to top it all off—got married at Disney World.

This added up to what they described as an 'unsustainable' lifestyle, where they were spending money as fast as they were making it, leaving little left over to invest and build wealth. Despite their high incomes, they had accumulated over $10,000 in credit card debt by 2012.

When Joel's wife had a car accident, they took it as their financial wake-up call and took that opportunity to create a host of new financial habits. Thankfully Joel's wife was fine, but the car was not. They decided they would not replace her car and instead became a one-car household, instantly freeing up hundreds of dollars per month from their monthly budget. That allowed them to take the $10,000 in insurance money, open an account with Vanguard, and started building a portfolio of low-cost index funds.

They created a habit of regularly talking about money and looking for ways to spend less and invest more. They gave up their expensive habit of buying electronic gadgets at BestBuy, canceled their cable subscription, and invested time in learning how to cook. They turned cooking into a regular habit, which allowed them to cut out all the money they wasted eating out and paying for meal kit services.

These changes didn't happen all at once: it takes time to change your habits, especially if you have a lot of habits that need changing. One year after the accident, they had cut their annual spending from over $100,000 to $60,000. In year two, they cut their spending down to $40,000. At the height of their saving streak, they were saving and investing 85% of their take-home pay.

Budgeting is a lot like dieting. Extreme diets that completely deprive you of ever having 'treats' is unsustainable. Depriving yourself of ever having a piece of cake for the rest of your life is not sustainable for most people. Neither is depriving yourself of every small expense or comfort in your life. They did not save 85% of their income for long—that level of frugality was simply unsustainable —but by temporarily cutting all non-essential spending, they were able to figure out what expenses they valued most. For example, they could live without the $100+ monthly cable bill, but cutting Netflix was a bridge too far.

Eventually, they leveled out at a sustainable level of spending, where they still spent money on what they valued most while investing a substantial amount. By the end of 2017, they were able to reach financial independence, covering their cost of living from their investments, and were able to spend more time doing what made them happy.

Joel and his wife went from $10,000 in credit card debt to financial independence in a little over five years by replacing bad financial habits with good ones and experimenting with their budget to find the balance between value-driven spending and investing a large percentage of their income.

Even if your income is not where you would like it to be, developing good financial habits is essential to building wealth. An investing strategy as simple and passive as investing in index funds is very scalable. The process is the same whether you are investing $100 or $1 million; if you build strong financial habits early in life when your income is relatively low, you will know exactly what to do with greater amounts of money as your income grows in the future.

Make money serve you

Throughout this book, I've given you all the tools required to be a successful long-term investor and build wealth. In this final chapter, you'll learn the most important lesson: how to use money and wealth to maximize your happiness, free up more of your time, and give you a sense of purpose and fulfillment.

Social comparison is the death of joy

If you compare yourself to others, making more money won't make you happier. Sadly, that is precisely what most people do.

If your goal was to have $100,000 saved by the time you were 30, you would feel pretty pleased with yourself if you pulled it off – that is until you found out that your best friend has $250,000 saved. If the subject ever came up in conversation, you would tell your friend that you were happy for them, but on the inside you would feel that nagging tinge of jealousy and inadequacy. It's not that you don't want your friend to succeed, but you don't want to feel like you're being left behind.

A 2005 paper titled 'Income and well-being: an empirical analysis of the comparison income effect' studied a large sample of the German population to examine how changes in income impacted different people's levels of happiness.[1] Their findings paint a sad story; people have a bad habit of comparing themselves to people who are richer than they are.

Here's a summary of their findings.

- *Making more money did have a small effect on the average person's happiness.*
- *Making more money makes poor people happy but has less impact on rich people.*
- *The happiness someone experiences when their income increases was diminished when they were told that other people in the study had the exact same increase in income.*
- *The maximum level of happiness was achieved when people were told they had a high income compared to other people in the study.*
- *Poorer people in the group were less happy when they found out they make below-average income.*

Most people are happy when they feel like they are doing better than those around them. So, we seek out comparisons to others in hopes of feeling better about ourselves. In doing so, we often find the opposite effect; we end up comparing ourselves to people richer than us, making us miserable.

A 2021 study found that 'unconditional self-acceptance' played a significant role in reducing the frequency in which college students compare themselves to other people. There's an important distinction between self-acceptance and unconditional self-acceptance. It's easy to accept yourself when you get a promotion or make a brilliant investment, but accepting yourself after you get fired or lose a ton of money on an overly risky investment is what separates self-acceptance from unconditional self-acceptance.

So, how do you cultivate a sense of unconditional self-acceptance? Clinical psychologist Adia Gooden has some ideas.[2]

- *Forgive yourself.* Reflect (but don't dwell) on past mistakes. Learn from them and say out loud: 'I forgive myself.'
- *Stop criticizing yourself.* When you catch yourself in a moment of critical self-thought, flip the script and start thinking about what you admire most about yourself.
- *Stay connected with your friends.* To quote Adia Gooden: 'When we think there's something wrong with us, we tend to pull away from our relationships, and this isolation only exacerbates our feelings of unworthiness.' If it's been a long time since you've kept in touch with your closest friends, reach out to them and strike up a conversation. Normalize calling your friends just to say 'hi'.

It's a long journey, but the more deeply you accept yourself, the less likely you are to compare your financial situation to others, and you'll be more likely to stay focused on your own investment goals.

Money buys you freedom, and freedom buys happiness

I don't want to give you the impression that money can't buy happiness because it absolutely can; it just does so indirectly. Money buys the one thing every human being in history has desired: freedom.

If you use money to buy freedom instead of cars, gadgets, and designer clothes, then more money will bring more happiness. You may have heard the statistic that happiness peaks once someone makes $75,000 per year; making money beyond this threshold will not make you happier. This so-called $75,000 happiness plateau comes from a 2010 paper by Daniel Kahneman, which measured the impact of income on two separate measurements of 'well-being' or happiness.[3]

- **Emotional well-being,** which is your daily feelings of joy, stress, sadness, anger, etc.
- **Life evaluation,** which is when you stop and look at the big picture of your life and ask yourself questions like 'Am I satisfied with where my life is going?'

Kahneman found that there was no clearly defined threshold for the impact of income on life evaluation; the study also revealed that emotional well-being did, in fact, plateau at around $75,000 per year.

Given the stature of Daniel Kahneman and the easy-to-digest narrative, it was widely interpreted that having more money won't buy you more happiness. Which, if you have never had to truly worry about money in your life, might be true. But anyone who has lived without money and then found themselves with lots of it knows that money—and specifically the freedom it affords us—absolutely makes us happier.

In a 2021 paper titled 'Experienced well-being rises with income, even above $75,000 per year', author Matthew Killingsworth challenged Kahneman's conclusion that happiness plateaus at $75,000 per year.[4] Killingsworth gave 33,000 people who participated in the study an app that collected real-time data on well-being. Participants were randomly asked to fill out brief surveys throughout the day; the app collected over 1.7 million responses that measured day-to-day happiness. By collecting enough snapshots of people's lives over time, you begin to build a clearer picture of what makes them happy.

The major finding was that making more money improves happiness whether you make more or less than $75,000. There is no defined threshold where suddenly making more money becomes meaningless.

Killingsworth believes that more money continues to make us happier because having more money allows us to have more control over how we live our lives. Consider two people looking for a job; one has $800 in the bank, and the other has $1 million. The millionaire can afford to turn down jobs until they find the right one. The person with $800 will have to take whatever job comes their way, even if it makes them miserable.

The more money you have, the more often you can say no to things that make you unhappy. When you have enough money stashed away to cover the bills for a few months, you can say 'no thank you'. When you have enough money to cover your expenses for a year or more, you can say 'no'. Building a portfolio that can cover your living expenses in perpetuity gives you the rare luxury of saying 'f*ck no!' when someone asks you to do something you don't want to do.

Once you start investing, you can start building wealth and slowly gain more and more control over your life, choosing to engage in more of the activities that make you happy and passing on tasks that make you unhappy or stressed. That's what it means to have 'FU' money.

A happy life requires threading the needle between time and money

The two most important assets in life are time and money. The key to a successful, happy life is knowing when to trade one for the other. You'll likely have to spend your early adulthood trading your time for money. Every dollar you invest while you are young can be used to buy back time later in life.

The pinnacle of 'buying time' is when you reach financial independence and doing any kind of paid work becomes optional. Financial independence is a great goal, but to be brutally honest, getting there might take several decades. Let's assume the following.

- *You're 30 and just started investing.*
- *You make $50,000 per year after tax.*
- *Your annual living expenses are $40,000.*

That leaves you with $10,000 per year to invest. If your investments earn 6% per year on average, then by the time you are 63, you will have a little over $1 million saved. If you followed the 4% rule and withdrew 4% of your portfolio to fund your lifestyle, you'd be able to live off $40,000 per year from your portfolio. It would take 33 years to reach financial independence – assuming everything went right.

Of course, these numbers would look a whole lot friendlier if you started investing earlier or had more money to invest, which you will as you advance through your career. However, the point stands: financial independence can be a lifelong pursuit.

But here's what most people miss about wealth: using money to buy time is not an all-or-nothing proposition. Yes, it may take a long time to get to the point where work becomes optional, but there will be lots of opportunities to buy back smaller chunks of your time as your income and wealth increase over the years.

Start with buying back a few hours per month
Everybody knows how expensive it is to buy and own a home. Between the down payment, lawyer and realtor fees, taxes, annual maintenance costs, and renovations —not to mention the cost of filling a house with furniture —it adds up very quickly.

Few people will tell you how much time your house steals from you. When my wife and I bought our house, one of the features that we loved most about the house was the big back yard. We envisioned endless barbecues, campfires, and summer days spent lounging in hammocks. While we have got to enjoy those things, I've spent more time in the garden pulling weeds, cutting the grass, and raking leaves. The more time you spend doing chores, the less time you have left to spend doing what makes you happy.

A 2011 paper titled 'The American Dream or The American Delusion?' written by Grace Bucchianeri examined the relationship between homeownership and happiness.[5] The study explored two questions about homeownership.

1. *Does becoming a homeowner make someone more or less happy?*
2. *How much time does a homeowner spend doing work around the house versus community activities and leisure activities?*

To quote Bucchianeri: 'After controlling for household income, housing quality, and personal health, homeowners were no happier than renters. **In fact, they derived more pain from their home than renters.'** Homeowners spend more time engaged in home maintenance tasks and less time out of the house having fun or visiting family and friends. It's impossible to overestimate how much time fixing even a 'small' problem around the house will cost you.

No free lunch: the opportunity cost of DIY home improvement projects.

My wife and I each work a full-time job, run a part-time business together, and have a very active toddler; we do not have much spare time. We're also homeowners, which means we spend most of our 'downtime' keeping the house in order. When our son was 18 months old, he used to take two-hour long naps in the middle of the day. On weekends, this two-hour window was one of the preciously few times my wife and I had time to relax and spend time together alone. One Saturday morning, the microwave died while I was reheating the same cup of coffee for the fifth time so that day I had to spend my son's nap time at Walmart buying a new microwave. The microwave was one of those 'over the range' ones that hang above your stove. This meant that on Sunday, we spent our son's nap time installing the microwave into the wall.

I am not a handy person; I hate any activity that requires a tape measure and screwdrivers. So, when we finished the installation, I felt no sense of pride in improving the quality of our home. I only felt momentary relief that the damn thing was in the wall. Within five minutes of completing the installation, our son woke up from his nap, and I was back on dad duties.

This is homeownership in a nutshell. Except, it doesn't have to be this way. Like many people, I was taught that paying someone else to do something you could do yourself—like pulling weeds or installing a microwave—is a waste of money and something that only pompous rich people do. Somewhere along the way, we misinterpreted being 'frugal' to mean never spending money. Yes, it's true that the less you spend, the more you can invest, build wealth, and reach financial independence. But don't lose sight of the fact that even for the biggest penny pinchers in the world, the path to financial independence is long. Pushing your timeline to financial independence from 33 years to 35 years might be worth it if you are spending money to buy back more time today.

A 2017 study titled 'Buying time promotes happiness' showed that spending money on time-saving services such as landscaping or housecleaning makes people happier.[6] This is especially true when you save time by avoiding a task you hate doing. Going back to my microwave installation, how much more enjoyable would my weekend have been if, instead of driving to Walmart, picking out a microwave and driving it home, and then installing it the next day, I simply bought one online and had it delivered and installed for me? Yes, there is a cost for this service, but the trap is thinking that doing these tasks yourself is 'free'. It costs you time, which is an even more scarce resource than money. This brings us back to the inescapable truth that happiness means knowing when to trade your time for money and vice versa.

What goes completely overlooked by most people is the benefits of spending money to buy back time and avoid doing tasks they despise. Somehow, we've convinced ourselves a $750 car payment is fine, but spending $125 for someone to clean your house top to bottom every month makes you careless with money, despite the evidence that suggests doing so could be the easiest way to increase your day-to-day happiness.

There is a word that describes the process of paying someone to do necessary tasks that you have neither the time nor the desire to do yourself: it's called delegating. Successful entrepreneurs understand the importance of delegation.

Take, for example, Richard Branson, the billionaire founder of The Virgin Group which owns 40 companies. Branson also has a personal stake in more than 400 other businesses. It would be literally impossible for him to be involved in the day-to-day operations of all of these businesses; part of what allowed him to generate a massive amount of wealth was by delegating tasks that sucked away his time.

As Branson said in a 2015 post on Virgin's blog, 'You need to learn to delegate so that you can focus on the big picture,' adding, 'It's vital to the success of your business that you learn to hand off those things that you aren't able to do well.'

You don't have to be a billionaire owner of a business conglomerate to realize that delegating certain tasks costs money, yes, but it also frees up time. Whether it's a good trade-off depends entirely on what you do with that time.

One effective way to use your newfound time is to get off your butt and out of the house. A 2019 paper titled 'Time Use and Happiness of Millionaires,' found that the way wealthy people use their time is what makes them happier than everyone else.

The study found that millionaires spend more time on 'active' leisure than 'passive' leisure. This means that millionaires spend 16 fewer minutes per day 'relaxing' and a further 16 fewer minutes watching TV, while spending 19 more minutes exercising and 8.3 more minutes volunteering than non-millionaires.

This additional time spent on active leisure as opposed to passive leisure (like watching Netflix) had a tremendous impact on the happiness of millionaires. This is encapsulated perfectly with this quote from the paper: 'The gap in happiness between the wealthy and the rest of us is similar to the reduction in happiness that occurs immediately after a divorce.'

Delegating tasks you dislike and reinvesting that time in active leisure can have a two times return on happiness. If, instead of spending my weekend installing a microwave, I went for a run in the park, I would have been much happier and energized on Sunday night.

Another good use of the time you free up through delegating household tasks is to spend that time making more money. If you run a business or have a side hustle, you could spend your time working and generating income. If you pay $125 for a house cleaner, and that frees up two hours that you can use to work and generate $300 in income, you come out ahead. This is the mindset of a wealthy business owner; paying to free up time is not a cost. It is an investment that can have serious ROI. And you may even get bonus happiness points if you enjoy working on your business or side hustle more than the task you delegated.

Buying back your workdays

The research paper studying how millionaires spend their time had another finding that demonstrated how freedom and control over our lives increases our happiness; wealthy people have much more control over how they spend their workdays. Wealthy people spent 93% of their work time deciding what to do and how to do it, compared to only 76% for the general population.

As you continue investing and accumulating wealth, you become less dependent on your paycheck to pay the bills. This, in turn, can provide you leverage to negotiate with your employer for higher pay and greater levels of autonomy in your job.

When I first started my 'career job' after grad school, I was deeply in debt and was financially supporting family members. I went to work every day with massive anxiety about getting fired. There was no reason to suggest I would get fired—every performance review was glowing—but still, the irrational fear was there because the consequences of getting fired would have been so severe that it led me to ruminate over a future that never came to pass.

A funny thing happened; as the years went by and I kept saving and investing more and more, I became less and less anxious about losing my paycheck. By the time I became a millionaire, I had already negotiated with my employer that I would work from home full time. That saved me over 10 hours per week in commuting time, thousands per year in saved gas and car maintenance, and the autonomy to do my work how I saw fit from the comfort of my home. The more wealth you have, the more of your workday you can buy back.

Buying back years
As we have already discussed, the most useful way to measure wealth is not how much money you have; it's how much money you have relative to your cost of living. This is the only calculation that matters when it comes to buying time back because it reveals how many years your current wealth could sustain your lifestyle.

If you are happy living on $40,000 per year and have $400,000 saved, you have enough money to buy 10 years of freedom. For every additional year of freedom your money can buy, you gain more control over your decisions. This, in turn, makes you happier. If you're not motivated by creating wealth, then you should focus on what that wealth is best used for: buying more freedom and optionality in your life.

Buy back every day you have left
Eventually, if you consistently save a healthy percentage of your income and invest in a diversified portfolio, you will reach financial independence, the point where you have enough wealth that you no longer need to work

to pay for your lifestyle. It's at this point you can buy back every day you have left on this earth and spend those days doing what you want, when you want, with whom you want.

If you've taken your time along the way to know how you want to spend your days, who you want to spend time with and where you want to live, then a happy, fulfilled life is what you will have. This is the dream of nearly everyone and is one of the most powerful reasons to embrace long-term investing. But as we just covered, financial independence is not the only way to buy back more of your time.

Don't make your whole life about a never-ending pursuit of a goal that might take 40 years to achieve. Have it as a goal, put a plan in place to make it happen, and then get on with the business of living a good life each day. Being afraid to live today in fear of not having enough in the future is just as bad as living only for today while neglecting your future.

It's about balance. Make strategic trade-offs along the road to financial independence that can buy you pockets of time while you are young enough to enjoy it. So many parents never take a week off to take their kids on vacation and build family memories; instead, they keep their nose to the grindstone, work non-stop and invest every single penny they earn so that one day they can have all the time in the world. The sad irony is that by the time they have all the time in the world, their children are grown and are spending their time starting their own families.

Building wealth is great, and reaching financial independence is amazing but don't be afraid to pick your spots and live along the way. The wise, wealthy, and happy investor understands when to trade time for money and when they have enough to start trading money for time.

Glossary

Arbitrage: Exploiting the difference in price of an identical asset in different markets.

Asset allocation: Deciding how much of your portfolio is invested in different assets.

Assets under management (AUM): The total market value of the investments a financial advisor manages on behalf of their clients.

Bear market: When a market experiences a prolonged price decline.

Bonds: An investment where the investor loans money to a borrower.

Bull market: When a market experiences a prolonged price increase.

Buy-and-hold: An investment strategy where an investor holds on to their investment for the long term, regardless of current market conditions.

Checking account (known as a current account in the UK): A bank account designed for daily deposits and withdrawals.

Dow Jones Industrial Average: One of the oldest stock market indices in the world consisting of 30 notable publicly traded companies in the US.

Down payment (known as a deposit in the UK): The money a buyer pays against the final price of a home or other large purchase.

Efficient market hypothesis: The theory that current stock prices reflect all available information, thus making it nearly impossible to consistently 'beat the market'.

Exchange traded fund (ETF): An investment fund that can be bought and sold on a stock exchange.

Finfluencer: An individual with a large social media following that can influence their followers' financial decisions.

Gross Domestic Product (GDP): The total value of the goods and services produced in a particular country in a particular year.

Idiosyncratic risk: Risk that is specific to a particular asset or group of assets.

Index funds: An investment fund designed to track a particular market index.

Leverage: Borrowed money used to invest.

Management expense ratio (MER): A fee paid by investors for the privilege to invest in a particular investment fund.

Nasdaq index: A market cap-weighted index (where companies are weighted according to market value of their shares) of 3,700 companies which is weighted towards the technology sector.

Options: A contract giving the holder the right—but not the obligation—to buy or sell an asset at a specific price on or before a specific date.

Portfolio: A collection of different investments like stocks and bonds.

Recession: A prolonged period of economic decline.

Retirement planning: The process of arranging your finances today so that you can maintain your standard of living in the future once you stop working.

Risk premium: The difference in return between a risky asset and a risk-free asset.

Robo-advisor: An automated investment service that makes algorithmic-based investment decisions on an investor's behalf.

Stocks (also known as equities): A share of ownership in a company.

Stock picking: The process of selecting individual stocks that an investor believes will outperform the general stock market.

S&P 500: A market cap-weighted index of the 505 largest publicly traded companies in the US.

Surrender charge: A fee levied upon an insurance policyholder upon cancellation.

Systematic risk: Risk that is inherent to an entire market.

References

Chapter 1:
1. Caporal, J., 'Gen Z and Millennial Investors: Ranking the Most Used, Trusted Investing Tools', The Motley Fool (3 Aug 2021).
2. Kienzler, M., Västfjäll, D. and Tinghög, G., 'Individual differences in susceptibility to financial bullshit', Journal of Behavioral and Experimental Finance, vol. 34 (June 2022)
3. Chinco, A., 'The Ex Ante Likelihood of Bubbles', Management Science (4 May 2022).

Chapter 2:
1. US Stock Market Returns - a history from the 1870s to 2022', The Measure of a Plan (themeasureofaplan.com)
2. Saad, L., 'What Percentage of Americans Owns Stock?', Gallup (13 September 2019).
3. Choi, J.J. and Robertson, A., 'What Matters to Individual Investors? Evidence from the Horse's Mouth', SSRN (30 September 2019).

Chapter 4:
1. 'Celebrating 20 Years', SPIVA - S&P Dow Jones Indices.
2. Chague, F., De-Losso, R., and Giovannetti, B., 'Day Trading for a Living?', SSRN Electronic Journal (22 July 2019).
3. Ibid.
4. 'Retail inflows at nearly all-time high despite market turbulence', Reuters (www.reuters.com).
5. de Silva, T., Smith, K., and So, E. C., 'Losing is Optional: Retail Option Trading and Earnings Announcement Volatility', SSRN Electronic Journal (29 July 2022)

Chapter 5:
1. Vanguard Portfolio Allocation Models, Vanguard.
2. 'A tale of two decades for U.S. and non-U.S. equity: Past is rarely prologue', Vanguard Research (December 2020).
3. Sharpe, W. F., 'The Arithmetic of Active Management', Financial Analysts Journal, 47(1), (1991), pp. 7 - 9.

Chapter 7:
1. Goetzmann, W. N. and Kim, D. 'Negative Bubbles: What Happens After a Crash', National Bureau of Economic Research, 1 September 2017. www.nber.org/papers/w23830#::text=We%20study%20crashes%20using %20data
2. 'Focus on time in the market, not market timing', Merrill Edge. www.merrilledge.com/article/focus-on-time-in-market-not-market-timing
3. 'Mind the Gap: A report on investor returns in the U.S.', Morningstar. www.morningstar.com/lp/mind-the-gap.

Chapter 8:
1. Will Storr, The Unpersuadables: Adventures with the Enemies of Science (The Overlook Press, 2014).
2. Thaler, R. H., 'Mental accounting matters', Journal of Behavioral Decision Making, vol. 12(3), 19 July 1999, pp.183-206. doi.org/10.1002/(SICI)1099-0771(199909)12:3 183:AID-BDM318 3.0.CO;2-F
3. Thaler, R. H., Tversky, A., Kahneman, D., and Schwartz, A., 'The Effect of Myopia and Loss Aversion on Risk Taking: An Experimental Test', The Quarterly Journal of Economics, vol. 112(2), pp. 647-661. doi.org/10.1162/003355397555226
4. Dunning, D. and Kruger, J., 'Unskilled and Unaware of It: How Difficulties in Recognizing One's Own Incompetence Lead to Inflated Self-Assessments', Journal of Personality and Social Psychology, vol. 77(6), January 2000, pp. 1121-34. www.researchgate.net/publication/12688660_Unskilled_and_Unaware_of_It_How_Difficulties_in_Recognizing_One

5. Dunning, D., 'We Are All Confident Idiots', Pacific Standard, 27 October 2014. psmag.com/social-justice/confident-idiots-92793

6. O'Donoghue, T. and Rabin, M., 'Doing It Now or Later', The American Economic Review, vol. 89(1), March 1999, pp 103-124. www.jstor.org/stable/116981

7. Henriques, D. B., 'Bernard Madoff, Architect of Largest Ponzi Scheme in History, Is Dead at 82', New York Times, 14 April 2021. www.nytimes.com/2021/04/14/business/bernie-madoff-dead.html

8. Chen, H.-Y., Chen, H.-C., and Lai, C. W., 'Internet search, fund flows, and fund performance', Journal of Banking & Finance, vol. 129(106166), August 2021. doi.org/10.1016/j.jbankfin.2021.106166

9. Tversky, A. and Kahneman, D, 'Judgment under Uncertainty: Heuristics and Biases', Science, vol. 185(4157), 27 September 1974, pp. 1124-1131. www.science.org/doi/10.1126/science.185.4157.1124

10. Essential Intelligence to Make Decisions with Conviction, 2018. S&P Global. https://www.spglobal.com/en/

11. JP Morgan, 'Is it worth considering investing at all-time highs?', Top Market Takeaways, 28 August 2020. www.jpmorgan.com/content/dam/jpm/securities/documents/cwm-documents/Is-it-worth-considering-investing-at-all-time-highs.pdf

12. '10 Things You Should Know About Bear Markets', Hartford Funds. www.hartfordfunds.com/practice-management/client-conversations/managing-volatility/bear-markets.html#:~:text=There%20have%20been%2026%20bear%20markets%20since%20201929%2C%20but,15%20recessions%20during%20that%20time.&text=Bear%20markets%20often%20go%20hand,mean%20a%20recession%20is%20looming.

13. Kelly, R., 'Familiarity Bias: Are You Your Greatest Enemy?', Yeske Buie, 2 September 2021. yebu.com/financial-planning/familiarity-bias-are-you-your-greatest-enemy#:~text=Familiarity%20bias%20is%20the%20idea

Chapter 9:

1. Puri, M. and Robinson, D., 'Optimism and economic choice', Journal of Financial Economics, vol. 86(1), October 2007, pp. 71-99. doi.org/10.1016/j.jfineco.2006.09.003

2. Plomin, R., Scheier, M. F., Bergeman, C. S., Pedersen, N. L., Nesseloade, J. R., and McClearn, G. E., 'Optimism, pessimism and mental health: A twin/adoption analysis', Personality and Individual Differences, vol. 13(8), August 1992, pp. 921-930. doi.org/10.1016/0191-8869(92)90009-e

3. Robb, K. A., Simon, A. E., and Wardle, J., 'Socioeconomic Disparities in Optimism and Pessimism', International Journal of Behavioral Medicine, vol. 16(4), May 2009, pp. 331-338. doi.org/10.1007/s12529-008-9018-0

4. Mindfulness exercises, Mayo Clinic (15 September 2020). www.mayoclinic.org/healthy-lifestyle/consumer-health/in-depth/mindfulness-exercises/art-20046356

5. Koopmann-Holm, B., Sze, J., Jinpa, T., and Tsai, J. L., 'Compassion meditation increases optimism towards a transgressor', Cognition and Emotion, vol. 34, 26 August 2019, pp. 1-8. doi.org/10.1080/02699931.2019.1703648

6. Mindfulness exercises, Mayo Clinic (15 September 2020). www.mayoclinic.org/healthy-lifestyle/consumer-health/in-depth/mindfulness-exercises/art-20046356

7. Seligman, M. E. P., Steen, T. A., Park, N., and Peterson, C., 'Positive Psychology Progress: Empirical Validation of Interventions'. American Psychologist, vol. 60(5), 2005, pp. 410-421. doi.org/10.1037/0003-066x.60.5.410

8. Littman-Ovadia, H., and Nir, D., 'Looking forward to tomorrow: The buffering effect of a daily optimism intervention', The Journal of Positive Psychology, vol. 9(2), 28 October 2013, pp. 122-136. doi.org/10.1080/17439760.2013.853202

9. Buchanan, K., Aknin, L. B., Lotun, S., and Sandstrom, G. M., 'Brief exposure to social media during the COVID-19 pandemic: Doom-scrolling has negative emotional consequences, but kindness-scrolling does not', PLOS ONE, vol. 16(10), 13 October 2021, e0257728. doi.org/10.1371/journal.pone.0257728

10. Peters, M. L., Flink, I. K., Boersma, K., and Linton, S. J. 'Manipulating optimism: Can imagining a best possible self be used to increase positive future expectancies?' The Journal of Positive Psychology, vol. 5(3), January 2010, pp. 204-211. doi.org/10.1080/17439761003790963

11. Miller F. E., 'Challenging and changing stress-producing thinking', Western Journal of Medicine, vol. 174(1), January 2001, pp. 49-50. www.ncbi.nlm.nih.gov/pmc/articles/PMC1071234/

12. 'Resilience', American Psychological Association, 2012. www.apa.org/topics/resilience
13. Carver, C. S., Scheier, M. F., and Segerstrom, S. C., 'Optimism', Clinical Psychology Review, vol. 30(7), November 2010, pp. 879- 889. doi.org/10.1016/j.cpr.2010.01.006
14. Sun, H., Tan, Q., Fan, G., and Tsui, Q., 'Different effects of rumination on depression: key role of hope', International Journal of Mental Health Systems, vol. 8, 13 December 2014. doi.org/10.1186/1752-4458-8-53
15. Hilt, L. M. and Pollak, S. D., 'Getting Out of Rumination: Comparison of Three Brief Interventions in a Sample of Youth', Journal of Abnormal Child Psychology, vol. 40(7), 22 April 2022, pp. 1157-1165. doi.org/10.1007/s10802-012-9638-3

Chapter 10:

1. Kahneman, D., Thinking, Fast and Slow (Farrar, Straus & Giroux, 2011).
2. Tronier, R. M., 'America's Love for Impulse Spending is Going Strong in 2022', Slickdeals Money, 19 May 2022. money.slickdeals.net/surveys/slickdeals-impulse-spending-survey-2022/
3. Strömbäck, C., Lind, T., Skagerlund, K., Västfjäll, D., & Tinghög, G., 'Does self-control predict financial behavior and financial well-being?', Journal of Behavioral and Experimental Finance, vol. 14, June 2017, pp. 30-38. doi.org/10.1016/j.jbef.2017.04.002
4. Davydenko, M., Kolbuszewska, M., and Peetz, J., 'A meta-analysis of financial self-control strategies: Comparing empirical findings with online media and lay person perspectives on what helps individuals curb spending and start saving', PLOS ONE, vol. 16(7), 8 July 2021, e0253938. doi.org/10.1371/journal.pone.0253938
5. Charles Duhigg, The Power of Habit (Random House, 2012). charlesduhigg.com/the-power-of-habit/
6. Financial 180. Retrieved 20 September 2022 from fi180.com/
7. 'Financial Freedom in Less Than Five Years with Joel from FI 180', Bigger Pockets, 12 March 2018. www.biggerpockets.com/blog/biggerpockets-money-podcast-11-financial-freedom-in-less-than-five-years-with-joel-fi-180

Chapter 11:

1. Ferrer-i-Carbonell, A., 'Income and well-being: an empirical analysis of the comparison income effect', Journal of Public Economics, vol. 89(5-6), June 2005, pp. 997-1019. doi.org/10.1016/j.jpubeco.2004.06.003
2. Gooden, A., 'How to cultivate a sense of unconditional self-worth' (18 November 2020), Ideas.ted.com. ideas.ted.com/how-to-cultivate-a-sense-of-unconditional-self-worth/
3. Kahneman, D. and Deaton, A., 'High Income Improves Evaluation of Life but Not Emotional Well-Being', Proceedings of the National Academy of Sciences, vol. 107(38), 4 August 2010, pp. 16489-16493. doi.org/10.1073/pnas.1011492107
4. Killingsworth, M. A., 'Experienced well-being rises with income, even above $75,000 per year', Proceedings of the National Academy of Sciences, vol. 118(4), 18 January 2021. doi.org/10.1073/pnas.2016976118
5. Bucchianeri, G. W., 'The American Dream or the American Delusion? The Private and External Benefits of Homeownership for Women', SSRN Electronic Journal, 2011. doi.org/10.2139/ssrn.1877163
6. Whillans, A. V., Dunn, E. W., Smeets, P., Bekkers, R., and Norton, M. I., 'Buying time promotes happiness', Proceedings of the National Academy of Sciences, vol. 114(32), 24 July 2017, pp. 8523-8527. doi.org/10.1073/pnas.1706541114
7. Bloomberg Billionaires Index, Bloomberg UK. Retrieved 22 September 2022 from www.bloomberg.com/billionaires/profiles/richard-c-branson/?leadSource=uverify%20wall
8. Clarkson, N., 'Richard Branson: Why delegation is crucial to success', Virgin. www.virgin.com/about-virgin/latest/richard-branson-why-delegation-crucial-success
9. Smeets, P., Whillans, A., Bekkers, R., and Norton, M. I., 'Time Use and Happiness of Millionaires: Evidence From the Netherlands', Social Psychological and Personality Science, vol. 11(3), 25 June 2019, pp. 295-307. doi.org/10.1177/1948550619854751

Index